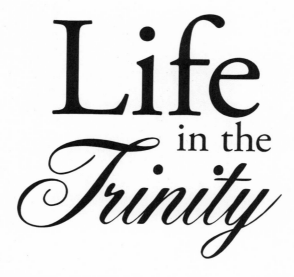

# Life
## in the
## *Trinity*

A Catholic Vision of Communion and Deification

# PHILIP KRILL

Cover icon: The Hospitality of Abraham by Andrei Rublev, 1424. Location: Tretyako Gallery, Moscow, Russia. Used with permission.

Scripture quotations marked RSV are taken from the Revised Standard Version of the Bible, copyright © 1946, 1952, 1971 by the Division of Christian Education of the National Council of the Churches of Christ in the USA. Used by permission.

ISBN: 978-1-4834-7380-2 (sc)
ISBN: 978-1-4834-7379-6 (e)

Because of the dynamic nature of the Internet, any web addresses or links contained in this book may have changed since publication and may no longer be valid. The views expressed in this work are solely those of the author and do not necessarily reflect the views of the publisher, and the publisher hereby disclaims any responsibility for them.

Any people depicted in stock imagery provided by Thinkstock are models, and such images are being used for illustrative purposes only. Certain stock imagery © Thinkstock.

Lulu Publishing Services rev. date: 08/22/2017

To

**Sister Peter Claver (Hannah) Fahy, MSBT**
**1899-2004**

+

who taught me the importance of prayer
and
showed me the love of the Trinity

# OTHER BOOKS BY PHILIP KRILL

Beyond the Foundation of the World:
Encountering the Trinity in Ephesians 1

Deified Vision: Towards an Anagogical Catholicism

*Gaudete:* Mysteries of Joy

The Hope of Glory: A Contemplative Reading of Colossians 1

More than Conquerers: The Pauline Mysticism of Romans 8

# Deification

We have been given exceedingly great and precious promises, that through these we may become partakers of the divine nature…

*~2 Peter 1:4*

The Son of God became what we are in order to make us what he is in himself.

*~ St. Irenaeus (d. 200)*

The Word became man that you may learn how it is possible for man to become God.

*~ St. Clement of Alexandria (d. 216)*

God became man that we might become God.

*~ St. Athanasius (d. 373)*

He gave us divinity, we gave him humanity.

*~ St. Ephrem the Syrian (d. 373)*

What is not assumed is not healed.

*~ St. Gregory Naziansius (d. 389)*

He became a partaker in our weakness, bestowing on us a participation in His divinity.

*~ St. Augustine (d. 430)*

The only-begotten Son of god, wanting to make us sharers in his divinity, assumed our nature, so that he, made man, might make men gods.

*~ St. Thomas Aquinas (d. 1274)*

# WITNESSES

My life has no other meaning than praising and contemplating the unique and total mystery of the Trinity.

~*Abbe Monchanin*

Let us lose ourselves in the Holy Trinity...who inclines Himself to us day and night, longing to impart Himself to us, to infuse His divine life into us, so as to make us deified beings, able to radiate Him everywhere.

~*Elizabeth of the Trinity*

...without Trinitarian thinking, one does not understand the first statement about Jesus or about the historical and temporal horizon of his human existence

~*Hans Urs von Balthasar*

# CREED

So, following the saintly fathers, we all with one voice teach the confession of the same Son, Our Lord Jesus Christ: the same perfect in divinity and perfect in humanity, the same truly God and truly man, of a rational soul and body; consubstantial with the Father as regards his divinity, and the same consubstantial with us as regards his humanity; like us in all respects except for sin; begotten before the ages from the Father as regards his divinity, and in the last days the same for us and for our salvation from Mary, the virgin God-bearer as regards his humanity; one and the same Christ, Son, Lord, only-begotten, acknowledged in two natures which undergo *no confusion, no change, no division, no separation*; at no point was the difference between the natures taken away through the union, but rather the properties of both natures is preserved and comes together in a single person and a subsistent being; he is not parted or divided into two persons, but is one and the same only-begotten Son, God, Word, Lord Jesus Christ, just as the prophets taught from the beginning about him, and as the Lord Jesus Christ himself instructed us, and as the creed of the fathers handed it down to us.

*Fourth Ecumenical Council of Chalcedon (ad. 451)*

# Contents

# PART ONE

# Divine Personhood

*Section One*

# *Trinity*

# HERMENEUTIC OF LOVE

*T*he Trinity is the Source, Goal (*Telos*), and Archetype (pattern) of everything that exists and can be known. All relationships among persons and things can be adequately understood and appreciated only in light of the Persons of the Most Holy Trinity. Human personhood finds its form, genesis, and fulfillment in Divine Personhood. On a practical level this means that all attraction, desire, communication, and communion that exist between and among human persons derives in one way or another from their relationship with the Divine *Hypostases* (Persons) within the unfathomable Mystery of the Blessed Trinity. Trinitarian personhood "lies at the root of all that exists."[1]

These are astounding claims. They fly in the face of what St. Paul has aptly described as the "wisdom of this world" (1 Cor. 3:19). Upon what do they rest? They rest upon the words of Jesus: "I am the Way, the Truth, and the Life. No one comes to the Father but through Me" (Jn. 14:6). The Person of Jesus identifies Himself as the Truth. No Jesus, no truth. Know Jesus, know Truth. This identification is an affront to the "wisdom of men" (1 Cor. 2:5). But to those who believe, it is "the power and wisdom of God"(1 Cor 1:24), making them "children of God and heirs of the Kingdom of God" (Rom. 8:16-17).

"The men of this age" (1 Cor. 2:6) think faith obscures our apprehension of truth. What Pope John Paul II termed the "hermeneutic of suspicion" insists that doubt and skepticism are the best approaches

---

[1] Archimandrate Sophrony (Sakharov), *We Shall See Him* (Stravopegic Monastery of St. John the Baptist, 1988) 191, cited in Archimandrate Zacharias, *Christ, Our Way and Our Life: A Presentation of the Theology of Archimandrate Sophrony*, (South Canaan, PA: St. Tikhon's Seminary Press, 2003) 20.

to truth. He described Nietzsche, Freud, and Marx as the "masters of suspicion." For the "culture of death" that has adopted their assumptions, truth is thought to be something best approached by suspending our convictions and laying aside our deeply held beliefs. Mental and emotional neutrality are said to be required conditions for getting at the truth of things. The scientific method in the study of nature, and the historical-critical method in the study of theology, are interpretive (hermeneutic) frameworks based on these convictions. Psychoanalysis and political ideology are practices founded on more virulent strains of the hermeneutic of suspicion.

Without for a moment denying or minimizing the benefits of the scientific method for understanding both in science and theology, it is important to complement and correct the "hermeneutic of suspicion" with a "hermeneutic of love." A hermeneutic of love replaces skepticism and doubt with openness and trust. It replaces cynicism and suspicion with empathy and understanding. It sees all things as created with beauty and purpose by God. It sees the world as having the form of love. It sees the world as participating in the Triune love of God.

The Trinity must be approached with faith and loyalty if the things and persons in the world He has created are to be grasped in their ultimate truth, beauty, and goodness. For it is in God that "we live, and move, and have our being, (Acts 17:28) and it is only "in Your Light, O Lord, that we see light" (Ps. 36:9). Jesus is the light of the world (Jn. 1:4; 8:12). He is the *Logos* (Jn. 1:1) from which all other lights proceed, including the light of reason. Human reason grasps what it does because it is enabled to grasp things through the power of the *Logos* who "In the beginning was with God, and was God" (Jn.1:1).

The problem, of course, is that it takes an act of faith to see the act of faith as the condition for knowledge. No one can compel such faith. It is a gift from God that must be sought and desired. Faith seeking understanding ("hermeneutic of love") is fundamentally different from understanding seeking to justify faith ("hermeneutic of suspicion"). Contemplative joy and mystical intuition result from the former; agnosticism, atheism, and intellectual arrogance, from the latter. Only through faith empowered by love can we know things in the right way. As Hans Urs von Balthasar has said, "…only the person who is convinced that Jesus knows him personally can gain access to knowledge of him. And only the person who is confident of knowing him as he is can know that he is also known by him."[2] This claim is a stumbling block to many academics, and an exercise in folly to the cultural elites, but to those who believe, it is the "power and wisdom of God" (1 Cor. 1:24).

Let us raise our minds and hearts, therefore, unto the ineffable Mystery of the Triune God. In this we follow the early church tradition that insists, ""If you are a theologian you will pray truly; and if you pray truly you are a theologian."[3] Let us engage in what Hans Urs von Balthasar calls "a kneeling theology." Let us approach God on our knees. Let us pray ourselves into right thinking, not attempt to think ourselves into right believing. Our belief in the Mystery of the Trinity precedes, and is the condition for the possibility of, knowledge about anything. When we do this in earnest, we begin to see that all attraction, desire, and relationship existing within the world of human longing and desiring stem in one way or another from the love, attraction, and ecstatic communion existing within the Life of the Triune God. There is no excellence in the human realm that is not first within the Trinity.

What we call "love" has the "form" of the One who *is* Love, namely God (1 Jn. 4:16). God is a Trinity of Divine Persons, whose very communion is the "definition" of love. God, as a *Communio Personarum*, re-defines the "meaning" of love. Love is not an impersonal concept or an abstract quality. Love is a divine community of Persons: Father, Son, and Holy Spirit. The Mystery of the One-in-Three and the Three-in-One is the primordial Mystery constituting the meaning and definition of love.

In the past 25 years there has been an explosion of interest in Trinitarian theology. Intellectuals of every Christian denomination have professed a renewed fascination with the Mystery of the Triune God. Why, then, has more of this interest within the academy not

---

[2] Hans Urs von Balthasar, *Does Jesus Know Us? Do We Know Him?* (San Francisco: Ignatius Press, 1983) 6.
[3] Evagrius, *On Prayer* #61.

flowed over into the wider Christian community? Could it be that there are fewer and fewer theologians of the sort the Church Fathers envisioned? Could it be that our churches and universities are filled with thinkers whose speculative works widen the gap between theology and prayer instead of heal it? We stand with Karl Barth, Hans Urs von Balthasar, and Popes John Paul II and Benedict XVI, who assert the uniqueness of Revelation and the priority of Jesus Christ. Our Trinitarian theology must be exquisitely Christocentric and completely *pneumatological* (Spirit-driven). Only a contemplative Trinitarian vision based squarely on the tradition of the early Church Fathers is capable of satisfying hearts hungry for the contemplative and mystical depths of genuine Catholic Christianity.

Catholic theological method must look in two directions at once. It must first look heavenward in contemplative gaze upon the Triune Mystery. It must also look towards the earth, loving those created in the "image and likeness" of the Trinity, seeing and loving in them what we see and love in Christ. Our method is always both "*katalogical*" (from the top down) and "*analogical*" (from the bottom up). "'Ana-logically' the truth of the world points, from its triadic structure, to the truth of God, and...'[k]ata-logically' (from above) Christ reveals to us a God who is, in his inmost essence, constituted by Trinitarian love."[4] Even more importantly, our method must be driven by the beauty and objectivity of divine Revelation. As the Fourth Lateran Council (1215) declared, "...between the Creator and creature, however great the similarity, even greater is the dissimilarity to be noted." Natural theology alone cannot bring us into intimate contact with the Blessed Trinity. Christology is always more than "anthropology writ large." As Pope John Paul II and the Documents of Vatican II (*Gaudium et Spes*, 22) insist, "Christ reveals man to himself." Our hermeneutic of love, therefore, must issue from a prayerful contemplation of the Trinity that illumines and perfects our analogical attempts to understand the Mystery.

It will be clear by now that in order to know what it is to be truly

---

[4] Rodney A. Howsare, *Balthasar: A Guide for the Perplexed* (London: T&T Clark International, 2009) 73.

6

human, we must first enter into the Mystery of the Triune God. More specifically, we must continually contemplate the Incarnation. The only truly human being was, and is, Jesus Christ. He is both a divine person and a human being. We are not fully human until we are reborn in Christ. Only by recapturing a sense of His Divine Personhood, especially as understood by the Church Fathers, can we begin to fathom the mystery of becoming truly human persons.

Here again the "hermeneutic of love" is of central importance. The figure of Christ, as Balthasar reminds us, "is only visible and productive as long as it is considered with the eyes of faith."[5] The darkness of academic theology since the Enlightenment testifies to the fact that there is no value-neutral knowledge of Jesus. The quest for the historical Jesus "leaves us practically with a heap of ruins, the destruction of the figure attested to by the New Testament. It is almost beyond comprehension that Catholic theologians can maintain this schizophrenic attitude themselves and recommend their students both adhere to the Church's faith (which presupposes this figure) and to adopt their kind of 'knowledge' which dissolves the confession of faith."[6] This is precisely why St. Paul eschewed a purely historically-neutral or personally-disinterested view of Jesus. "Even though we once regarded Christ from a purely natural point of view" (*kata sarka*), Paul says, "we no longer do" (2 Cor. 5:16).. The divine beauty, truth, and goodness of Jesus Christ are revealed only to those who approach Him with loving faith. Our knowledge of Jesus is always a personal *encounter* with Jesus.

Images and icons found in both the Catholic and Orthodox traditions convey something of the depths of the Incarnation and the intimacy that obtains within the Trinitarian *Communio*. As I write these words, I am gazing upon the Vladimir Madonna: a Russian icon of the Blessed Virgin as she caresses the infant Savior, his face pressed to hers in an image of mutual adoration. We catch a glimpse here, not only the inseparable union of Jesus and Mary in the mysterious economy of

---

[5] Von Balthasar, ibid., 61.

[6] *Ibid.*, 65.

salvation,[7] but also of the Trinitarian glory. Not only does it move us, but it also somehow draws us into itself. In our journey into the Trinity, therefore, we want to join and enter into the divine intimacy we see manifest in the Vladimir icon.

Another icon by Andrei Rublev, known as the Old Testament Trinity, is perhaps an even more fontal example of Christian art partaking of, and showing forth, something of the Trinitarian *Communio*. Here we see three angels visiting Abraham at Mamre (Gen. 18:1-17) and sharing in his hospitality. Rublev depicts these angels as proto-typical figures of the Persons of the Trinity. Their *tri-forme* iconic intimacy draws the beholder into a heavenly embrace. The Son inclines towards the Father. The Father blesses the Son. Both Son and Father point towards the Holy Spirit. The Spirit inclines towards the Eucharist, positioned at the icon's center, as if the entire Trinitarian *Economia* were aimed at delivering this sacramental Mystery to humankind. Endless are the associations and inspirations we can receive by contemplating the Rublev masterpiece.[8]

In both icons mentioned here, we catch a glimmer of the Trinitarian Mystery. They disclose a vision of union, and invitation to intimacy, that is made possible only by and in Christ. They reveal a promise of communion with God, and with each other, into which every human person is called. As the *Catechism of the Catholic Church* says, "The desire for God is written in the human heart, because man is created by God and for God; and God never ceases to draw man to himself" (#27). All power of attraction, all desire for union, stem from our inseparable connection to the Trinitarian *Communio*. We desire to "be with" others because we share in the "being with" that defines the Persons of the Trinitarian *Communio Personarum*. The meaning of being human is found in our contemplation of, and union with, the Triune God.

---

[7] St. Irenaeus called Mary "the cause of salvation for herself and for the whole human race" in *Against Heresies*, 3, 22, 4, as found in Willam A. Jurgens, ed., *The Faith of the Early Fathers* (Collegeville, MN: Liturgical Press, 1970) Volume 1, n. 224.
[8] See Henri Nouwen's book on icons, *Behold the Beauty of the Lord: Praying with Icons* (Notre Dame, IN: 1987), especially the chapter on Rublev's "Hospitality of Abraham."

# THE TRIUMPH OF HYPOSTASIS

*W*ho is a person? What is a person? How is a person more than simply an individual example of the human species? These are the questions that occupy us now, as we move more deeply into our contemplation of the twin mysteries of Divine and human personhood.

To find our answers we must always return in contemplation of the Source of Divine Personhood: the Father, Son, and Holy Spirit – One God in Three Persons - Persons in perfect communion with Each Other from all eternity. As we have already said - but it bears repeating - the light of Faith, given us in Divine Revelation, illumines and makes possible the only true knowledge about the human person. "In Your light, O Lord, we see light" (Ps. 39:6). Our quest for the truth about the human person must always return to what the Triune God has revealed about Himself in the Incarnation. Jesus is "the Way, the Truth, and the Life" (Jn. 14:6). The mysterious, ecstatic, ineffable Communion of Persons (*Communio Personarum*) is the Source, Goal, and Archetype of everything that exists and can be known, especially regarding the mystery of human personhood. It is the incomparable glory of the Trinity that accounts for the beauty, truth, and goodness of all human relationships. There is no model or pattern for the proper relationship among or between persons, except that of the Trinitarian Communion.

It is exceedingly difficult, and requires a singular grace, to conceive of the Trinity primarily as a communion (*koinonia*) of ontologically distinct yet eternally inseparable Divine Persons. There are many reasons for this difficulty, not the least of which is that there exists a long philosophical and theological tradition describing God primarily as a Divine Substance (*ousia*). It would be impossible and counter-productive for the contemplative vision we seek to recount here the

9

multi-layered history of the Trinitarian debates over thinking about God as a Community of Persons (*Hypostases*) instead of as a Divine Substance (*ousia*). Both these important terms, *ousia* (substance, nature, essence, form) and *hypostasis* (person), have complex and difficult philological histories.[9] For the first three centuries of the Christological and Trinitarian controversies in the Church, the concepts of *hypostasis* and *ousia* tended to be used interchangeably. It was with the triumph of the term *Hypostasis* (Person), primarily in the writings of the Cappadocian Fathers, Sts. Gregory Nazianzus, Gregory of Nyssa, and Basil the Great, that made it possible to conceive of God fully and completely as a *Communio Personarum*.[10] This development was revolutionary and transformative for the future of theological reflection.

What do we mean when we say God is a *Communio Personarum* instead of a Divine Nature or Substance? What is at stake when we speak about God as a Community of Persons instead of as "the Ground of our Being" or "the Uncaused Cause"? The very nature of these questions suggests something of why the early Church Fathers were so much occupied by these issues. In debating and discussing the nature (*ousia*) of God, the Fathers asked themselves in many different ways: how can God be one in nature (*ousia*) yet different in person (*hypostasis*)? How can we account for the unity in God without short-changing or compromising the singularity of the individual Persons (*hypostases*)?

Taking the Cappadocians as our guide, we see that Personhood in God – and the "distance" and separateness (otherness) between and among Father, Son, and Holy Spirit - is *constitutive* of the unity of the Trinity, not consequent upon it. What this means is that God is not first one and then three. He is *simultaneously* one and three. Personhood

---

[9] For an excellent summary of the essence-substance-person debate from a western theological perspective, see Joseph Cardinal Ratzinger, "Concerning the Notion of Person in Theology," *Communio: International Catholic Review* 17 (Fall, 1990) 439-454. Ratzinger notes that the final formula of this mystery in the West was *una essential-tres personae*; Tertullian said, *una substantia-tres personae*, and Augustine *una essential-tres substantiae*.

[10] The Cappadocian Fathers are Sts. Gregory Nazianzus, Gregory of Nyssa, and Basil the Great.

and Otherness among the Persons of the Trinity is eternal, absolute, and ontological. God's nature as God, in other words, did not, does not, and never can nor will precede His being Three separate Persons. The very separateness of the divine Persons, in their distinct, unique, and utterly singular otherness from each other, *constitutes* ("makes," "creates" "causes to be") their unity (their "nature," their "oneness," their "unity," their "substance"). In other words, there is no substance, being, or nature (*ousia*) of God prior to, ancillary with, or in addition to His existence as Father, Son, and Spirit (*Hypostases*).

These are amazing claims. They fly in the face of much of conventional, and even eminent, speculation on the nature of God. They represent a personalist ontology that forever undermines and overthrows other, a more substantialist ontology that would have Being and God be somehow synonymous. God's identity is not Being-writ-large, nor is His unity ensured, as many theologians have believed, by emphasizing God's unity or substance.

Both God's unity and the otherness of the Trinitarian Persons is ensured by what the Cappadocians called the *Monarchia* of the Father. Though Himself one Person within the Trinity, the Father is the Source and Origin (*Arché*) of the other Trinitarian Persons. The Father is never without the Son, the Son never without the Father, and neither ever without the Holy Spirit. Yet, the Son and the Spirit proceed from the Father. The Father does not proceed from the Son or the Spirit. It is the personalist hierarchy within the Trinity, not a least common, substantial denominator (substance) existing among the Persons, that establishes and secures their inseparable unity.

Here we begin to glimpse the revolutionary difference between conceiving of God as Pure Act or Primary Mover and a Community of Persons. He is always and everywhere *only* Father, Son, and Holy Spirit. There is no common, pre-existing common "substance" or "essence" that unites the Persons of the Trinity or accounts for their each being God. There never was, is, nor will be any non-Trinitarian or trans-Trinitarian God. Generic monotheism is an impious affront to classical Trinitarian Christian theology.

It is spiritually arresting and transformative to realize that the otherness that exists among the Persons within the Trinity is absolute. It is revolutionary to our spiritual life to realize that there is no pure Being that precedes, under girds, or stands behind, the actual Persons of the Trinity. We must strive to appreciate ever more deeply the mystery that the Persons of the Trinity, in their unity, are not constituted by some more primordial Being. They are Who They Are. Their being *is* their Personhood. "Tell them 'I am Who Am,'" says Yahweh when Moses asks God's Name (Ex 3:14). The Father, Son, and Spirit are *absolutely different* (*diaphora*). They are always and forever "unmixed and unconfused," as Chalcedon reminds us. From all eternity none of the Trinitarian Persons has ever been subject to confusion with either of the other two. Their being does not precede their Communion. The unity of the Trinity consists of the unbreakable communion (*koinonia*) that exists between and among Father, Son, and Holy Spirit. [11]

This is simply another way of saying that the God of Abraham, Isaac, Jacob, and Jesus is not to be identified with the God of the philosophers. It's as if, pulling back the veil of created reality, we discover there, not the Prime Mover of Aristotle or even the Uncaused Cause of the Scholastics, but the Rublev Trinity: Father, Son, and Holy Spirit united in a communion of love, inviting the beholder to "come, have supper" with them (cf. Rev. 3:20). God cannot be grasped within any conceptual framework. "I am Who Am" (Ex. 3:14). God addresses man; man encounters God. God always is a Name – a "Thou" – a Trinity of Persons who also "calls man by name" (Isa. 43:1). God is never an object, simply to be discussed or made in any other way subject to the categories of human understanding. He is always and only a supremely personal *Communio Personarum,* calling, summoning, and inviting human persons into intimate relationship with Himself.

It is most important to stress that because Personhood within the

---

[11] "*The philosophical God is essentially self-centered, thought simply contemplating itself.* The God of faith is basically defined by the category of relationship." Joseph Cardinal Ratzinger, *Introduction to Christianity* (San Francisco: Ignatius Press, 1990) 147. For a detailed examination of Ratzinger's theological and anthropological personalism, see Miroslav Volf, *After Our Likeness* (Grand Rapids, MI: William B. Eerdmans Publishing Company, 1998) 29-67.

Trinity is *ontological, what* God is is identical with *Who* He Is. We cannot really conceive of God in terms of 'Being' at all. God is *beyond* or *without* being, as we understand it.[12] God *defines* what 'being' is; the concept

---

[12] See J-L Marion, *God Without Being*, (Chicago: University of Chicago Press, 1991) for a Catholic appreciation of this point. See also von Balthasar's discussion of "The Fourfold Distinction," in which he shows that both Being (*esse*) and beings derive their "existence" from a Power greater than themselves, i.e., the Triune God. "…Being as a whole or the actuality of all that is does not generate from itself the actual entities, for the responsible generation of forms would presuppose a conscious and free spirit…[namely] God [who] is the sole sufficient ground for both Being and the existent in possession of a form." *The Glory of the Lord: A Theological Aesthetics*, Volume 5 (San Francisco: Ignatius Press, 1991) 624.

At the same time, there are, in the Catholic world of theological reflection, inspiring 'arguments,' including those of Hans Urs von Balthasar, which present metaphysics (i.e., the 'Unity of Being' and the 'Dramatic Structure of Truth') as illuminative of, as well as derivative from, the Christological and Trinitarian Mysteries of the Faith. Especially edifying is D. C. Schindler's explication of Balthasar's distinction of beings [as a noun] (*essentiae*) from Being [as a verb] (*esse*). Not only do all beings ('things,' 'created essences') depend on Being (the Power-of-Be-ing, 'is-ing-ness'), but the reverse is also true: Being (esse, the Power of Be-ing), as complete and simple but non subsistent, does not subsist, thus it needs particular beings (essendi) 'in' which to become actual. As Balthasar puts it, "not only 'concepts without intuition are empty,' but the 'idea' or the 'light' or the 'abundance' of Being remains so too." See D. C. Schindler, *Hans Urs von Balthasar and the Dramatic Structure of Truth*.

In his remarkable book, *Gift and the Unity of Truth*, Antonio López relates this same 'real distinction' between Being (*esse, Sein*) and beings (*essentiae, Seinde*) to the distinctions between God and the world, the Creator and the creation, the intra-Trinitarian differences between Father, Son, and Spirit, and the Incarnation. "…Christ follows the path of being because at the Incarnation he recapitulates the way esse (*esse commune*) [Being] comes into being at the moment of creation as always already poured out into essences [*essentiae*.] The Incarnation of the Logos follows being's 'event' of becoming a finite singular. Created esse, as we saw, does not have a hypostatic existence of its own. It exists only as already given to the essence that limits it, while the essence exists only because esse is always already given to it. The act of creation is the simultaneity of esse (which preserves its real unity in a non-hypostatic way) being in essences and essences existing as a result of esse. As we saw, this is the event (not a movement) of be-ing in which the two poles exist always for and with each other. As Balthasar writes, 'The fact that being pours itself out into the plurality of creatures as both actual (*simplex et completum*) and non-subsistent and that it cannot be apprehended (let alone solidified in a concept) except in this

of "being" in no way defines or describes anything that can rightly be considered "of God."

Perhaps the most difficult challenge in writing a book like this is to consistently and adequately convey the all-important difference between primary and secondary causality: between, that is, God as *truly transcendent* and all other reality that is necessarily contingent. Forgetfulness about this irreconcilable difference has been the theological shoal upon which many an even learned thinker has foundered. Consider, for example, a cherished axiom of a respected Catholic theologian, attempting to show the difference between God and the world He created: "God determining or determined: there is no other alternative."[13] Notice how he speaks of God as a term *within a shared frame of causal operation*. But God is never a subject or an object as we understand or experience these terms. Once God is introduced as one of the terms within a shared frame of reference, the formula is immediately rendered vacuous. That is why much of scholastic philosophy and theology fails to inspire. If the reality of God as Person is to be truly apprehended, His transcendence, even as a concept, must be grasped according to

---

outpouring, reveals it to be the pure and free expression of the divine *bonitas* (goodness) and freedom.' Expressing all of his divine nature within the limits of human nature, the Incarnate recapitulates the gift of creation in which the *ipsum esse* (*simplex et completum*) subsistens limits itself, so to speak, in finite beings. The Word undergoes substantification by means of human nature, without changing his divine nature in any respect...We can press this point further: the hypostatic union recapitulates the structure of created in its dual unity not only because Christ follows the way of being - if it were just this, the Logos would lose his transcendence and his mission would remain meaningless. More importantly, it is also because being is created in Christ and for him. It is here that philosophy must let itself transcend into theology to discover therein its ultimate ground" (*Gift and the Unity of Being*, 153, 155). As brilliant as these correlations are, such an analysis still appears not to fully appreciate the Absolute Priority, Singularity and 'Otherness' of Christ. It is not simply that, as López states so well, "being is created in Christ and for him," but that "being" has no conceptual meaning or any kind of actual subsistence at all apart from Christ. Person precedes Being in the Trinity and in the Divine Economia.

[13] Reginald Garrigou-Lagrange, *Predestination: The Meaning of Predestination in Scripture and the Church,* trans. Dom Bede Rose (Rockford, Ill.: TAN Books and Publishers, Inc., 1998).

a rule enunciated by the early Church Fathers: Whereas the being of finite things has non-being as its opposite, God's "being" is entirely beyond ["other than"] any such opposition.[14] The reality of God's Trinitarian Life, in other words, transcends the dialectic of existence and non-existence altogether. God's "being" is "necessary," as the philosophers say, not only because it is inextinguishable or externally immune to nothingness, but because "it transcends even the distinction between finite act and finite potency, since both exist by virtue of their participation in God's infinite actuality, in which all that might be always super eminently *is*."[15]

Not only is God not in any sense determined by our understanding of what it means to exist, the very meaning of "is" and "is not" is defined by contemplation of the Trinitarian *Hypostases*. God's transcendence transcends even the traditional demarcation between immanence and transcendence. God is the "is" both of the "it is" and the "it is not." The Fountainhead of all that exists, the Trinity cannot be conceived of as a subsequent division of pre-existent Absolute Being. For God "to be" is for Him always and forever to be "Father, Son, and Spirit." He has no "being" apart from His Personal *Hypostases*. His essence (nature, substance) *is* the otherness and unconfused particularity of His three different *Hypostases*. His unity *is* the *koinonia* that obtains among Father, Son, and Holy Spirit. Being *IS* communion in God.[16]

All of what has been said thus far can be summarized simply by saying that God is a *Who*, never a *What*. Or better: God is a Community of Who's. He is a "family," so to say, of Divine, personal *Hypostases* whose very nature is to exist *only* in indissoluble and unconfused communion. These Three Persons constitute such an unbreakable unity (*communio*) that none of them can ever be conceived of as "existing" apart from the others. Yet, to describe them as "one God" implies no compromise

---

[14] See St. Maximus the Confessor, *Chapters on Love, III*, 65.

[15] David Bentley Hart, "Impassability as Transcendence," in James F. Keating and Thomas Joseph White, O.P., ed., *Divine Impassibility and the Mystery of Human Suffering* (Grand Rapids, MI: William B. Eerdmans Publishing Co., 2009) 300.

[16] See John Zizioulas, *Being as Communion* (Crestwood, NY: St. Vladimir Seminary Press, 1985).

of their separate hypostatic identities.. The 'oneness' in the immanent Trinity does not precede their otherness, whether considered logically, chronologically, or ontologically. On the contrary, the unity within God is *constituted by* their three-Person-ness from the very beginning. For God to "exist" is for Him to be always and forever *only* Father, Son, and Holy Spirit. This "unity-in-difference" is impossible to appreciate unless and until God reveals Himself as a community of Persons, inviting His beholders into *communio* with Himself.

I am aware of strangeness involved in these elliptical and asymmetrical (some may say 'roundabout' and 'confusing') ways of describing the Trinitarian Mystery. There is no other way, however, to go about the business of approaching God with intellectual integrity infused with respectful and reverent faith. The history of Christianity reveals many ways in which the nature and personhood of the Triune God can be ill-defined and gotten wrong, especially by intellects exercised without sufficient faith. For our part, we ought never attempt to describe the nature of God in ways that strip the Triune Mystery of its numinous, paradoxical glory.

We are not concerned here with having the final word about Subordinationism, Monarchianism, or any of the other Trinitarian disputes that so exercised the early church. We desire, rather, to contemplate the Mystery of the Trinity as described by the Councils of Nicea (325 a.d.) and Chalcedon (451 a.d.) We seek to recover a vision of the Triune God in which, as Athanasius says, "the Father is never without the Son, and the Son is never without the Father." This double negative is not unimportant. God in His glory cannot be apprehended except through oblique, untoward, and paradoxical ways of approaching His Trinitarian Majesty.

The mystery of the Trinity is paradoxical and ineffable from beginning to end. "I and the Father are one," says the Son (Jn. 10:30), while at the same time, "the Father is greater than I" (Jn. 14:28). Here we have the Trinitarian Mystery in an impenetrable nutshell. Jesus, His Father, and their Holy Spirit constitute an *ek-static* communion of love which is an eternal unity-in-difference. It is a unity-in-difference that respects, maintains, and reveals a corresponding difference-in-unity. The complementarity of the Three-in-One and One-in Three both transcends and transforms the minds and hearts of those who contemplate Him in prayerful adoration.

# UNITY-IN-DIFFERENCE

*J*f the *Hypostases* (Persons) of the Trinity are eternally unique and forever "unconfused," they are also, as Chalcedon puts it, "inseparable and undivided." If the Persons of the Trinity are absolutely "other" from all eternity, they are also forever interdependent. The Trinity forms the primordial *Communio Personarum* of "otherness in communion" and "communion in otherness." Their unity-in-difference is also, simultaneously and eternally, a "difference-in-unity."

In the previous section we have tried to show that Personhood constitutes the very *being* of God. To this end we noted that the Persons of the Trinity are not species of a more primordial genus called "God." The Trinitarian Persons are not instances or modes of a more fundamental, pre-existing Substance. Nor are they metastases of a prior Essence or Uncaused Cause called "God." Undifferentiated theism is an insult to Trinitarian contemplation. In this section, by way of supplement, we will now contemplate the other side of the Mystery. For if singular and separate Personhood constitutes the very being of God's *nature*, then *Communion* constitutes the nature and being of God's *Personhood*.

What are we saying? We are saying that Being is ontologically, absolutely, and eternally *personal* in God. "In the light of this mutual indwelling...'objectivity' disappears."[17] Or better, the 'objectivity' of God consists in the pure *personal subjectivity* of His three divine *Hypostases*. God's Trinitarian Existence is constituted by the fact that He is Three distinct *Persons*. To "be," for God, is to be *Person*. From all eternity God is *never not* a *Community of Persons*. Personhood in the Trinitarian

---

[17] Von Balthasar *Does Jesus Know Us? Do We Know Him?*, 53.

Life of God is always and forever "otherness in communion" and "communion in otherness."

Let us pause for a moment and ponder the infinite implications of these double negatives. The mysteries of both the Trinity and the Incarnation compel us to use them. Against the heretic, Arius, whose mantra about Christ was, "There was when he was not," St. Athanasius repeated what became the measure of Christological orthodoxy: "There was never a time when the Son was not." More than a denial of Arius' denial of Christ's divinity, Athanasius' phrase contains fathomless insight into the unique personalism of the Trinitarian *Communio*. For if there 'was never a time when the Son was not," there was also never a time when the Father was not the Father, That is, there was never a time when God's identity was anything other than Father, Son, and Spirit, forever sharing a mutually surrendering and receiving of their very Persons with each other. When St. John, therefore, says "God is love" (1 Jn. 4:16), he means that love is not a "something;" it is a Trinity of "Someone's." God is love, but all "love" is not God. Love, as we understand and experience it, reflects and participates in the Triune Communion of Persons. "Love" is not a pre-existing 'something' that the Persons of the Trinity share with each other. The form and 'substance' of love *is* the *Communio Personarum* of the Trinity. Whatever does not resemblSe or partake of the Trinitarian *Communio* cannot proper be called "love" at all.

To put the theological point more baldly: God the Father has no being outside His complete self-gift of Himself to the Son, expressed in an act of eternal begetting and generation. Similarly, but differently, the Son has no being other than His grateful and obedient, eternal, and kenotic (self-emptying, self-effacing) self-donation to His Father. The Father does not exist outside his act of giving himself to the Son, nor has the Son any "existence" apart from His eucharistic disposition of surrender in response to the Father's begetting of Him. Father and Son in their respective identities are held together as infinite and eternally inseparable Persons by the Holy Spirit who, as Himself a separate, inseparable Person, serves within the Triune *Communio* to facilitate and maintain the mutual self-giving of Father and Son.

One of the key mystical implications of the Trinitarian *Communio* is that the Son is, in a very real sense, internal to the Father's own essence.[18] No Son, no paternity of the Father. No paternity of the Father, no Persons-in-relation in the Trinity. "The Father could not be Father (and nothing but Father) unless the Son were always already internal to his divinity (as a distinct *hypostasis*, not as a part).[19]

To say, then, with Athanasius, that "there never was a time when the Son was not" is also to realize that the Son's Yes to the Father is *ingredient*, both to the Son's identity as Son and to the Father's identity as Father. One could say, with Adrienne von Speyr, "The Son even cooperates in his begetting by letting himself be begotten...[since] The Son prefers nothing to doing the Father's will, for even in being begotten he carries it out...The divine processions occur in eternal simultaneity," so that the Father's very act of begetting "is an act of surrender to the Son, to which the Son replies with surrender."[20]

The surrender of Christ on the Cross for the salvation of the world is but the time-bound manifestation of the posture He assumes in relationship to the Father from all eternity within the Trinity. Indeed, everything Jesus says and does in His Incarnation – from the smallest aspect of his earthly ministry to the most the graphic detail of His Paschal Mystery - can be seen as a visible, iconic expression of His eternally kenotic, obedient, and supremely grateful posture of self-surrender to the Father within the inner life of the immanent Trinity. As Balthasar tireless repeats, "it is impossible to make sense of the Incarnation and of the *kenosis* which it implies apart from the eternal *kenosis* of the three Persons of the Trinity."[21]

In a less mystical way, we can further illustrate what is at stake here by anticipating what we will explore later in more detail about the nature of *human* personhood. A human person is also a *hypostasis*

---

[18] Adrienne von Speyr, *The World of Prayer* (San Francisco: Ignatius Press, 1985) 57-70.
[19] Adrian J. Walker, "The Gift of Simplicity: Reflections on Obedience in the Work of Adrienne von Speyr," *Communio 34* (Winter, 2007) 576.
[20] Von Speyr, *The World of Prayer*, 59.
[21] John O'Donnell, S.J., *Hans Urs von Balthasar* (London: Geoffrey Chapman, 1992) 46.

(person) who *is constituted by* his or her *relationships* with others. Human personhood "emerges" in dialogue, interaction, and intercourse with others. Human persons are *ineluctably social* in nature. The human person is an "I" who develops and comes into "possession of himself" only in so far as he goes out towards, and relates to, others. Solipsism and ontological solitude are not options for the human person. No human person ever comes to be or develops fully in isolation from others. The human person only "comes to be" as an "I" by reaching out to, and encountering, a "Thou." *"I-Thou" is the divinely constituted form for being human.* In this it reflects and participates in the divinely social nature of the Trinitarian *Communio Personarum.*[22]

It is the presence of a "Thou" that affirms and enables the existence of an out-reaching "I." Only a "Thou" makes it possible for an "I" to experience oneself as a unique, unrepeatable, unsubstitutable, one-of-a-kind *hypostasis* (person). No human person can actualize or come into full possession of their incomparable and incommensurable identity without loving engagement with other persons. Love = engagement. Being and becoming for human persons are realized only in relationship. If we separate the "I" from the "Thou," the "I" loses its uniqueness. It loses, therefore, something of its very being. "To be" and "to be in relationship" are ontologically identical for the human person.

Trinitarian Persons, of course, do not "emerge" or "develop" as human persons do. Yet, their unique identities as incomparable and incommensurable Persons are just as much "constituted by" their *inter*dependent relationships as those of the human persons made in their image and likeness. Or, more properly: human persons are constituted by relationship with other persons *precisely because* Personhood in God is essentially, ineluctably, and eternally relational. If the "being" of the

---

[22] "In the biblical account, solitude is the way that leads to the unity that we can define, following Vatican II, as *communio personarum* (GS 12)…One could also use the term 'community' here, if it were not so generic and did not have so many meanings. *"Communio"* says more and with greater precision, because *it indicates precisely the 'help' that derives in some way from the very fact of existing as a person 'beside' a person."* John Paul II, *Man and Woman He Created Them: A Theology of the Body* (hereafter TB), trans. Michael Waldstein (Boston: Pauline Books and Media, 2006) 162-163.

Trinity consists in the relationality and communion that exists among and between the divine Persons, the being and becoming of human persons is likewise constituted by the need for relationality inscribed in our very bodies, hearts, minds, and souls.

The essential relationality that obtains within the life of the Trinity, then, is the source, goal, and form of all human "being-in-relationship." It is important to keep the proper order and perspective here. The kind of *communio* enjoyed by the Persons of the Trinity is the *divine template* for human relationships, not vice versa. It is easy, when trying to imagine how communion and otherness are integrated within the Trinitarian Mystery, to confuse Christology with anthropology. Communion within God is never simply human *koinonia* amplified and expanded. Still less are the Father and the Son ever to be seen as simply the highest example of human aspirations.

While avoiding these mistakes, it can nevertheless be helpful to contemplate relationality within the Trinity by comparing them with our human experiences of communion and otherness as we experience these under the conditions of sin. In our fallen state, we usually experience communion and otherness, love and freedom, as contradictory ideals. From our perspective as sinful creatures, these seem to be opposites and mutually exclusive qualities. The "other" is most often perceived as a threat to my own "autonomy." My "independence" seems to be compromised by the demands of others and the call for commitment. To be protected, my "individuality" needs, it seems, to be free from encroachment by others. My "need for space" appears to be secured only by keeping at arms length those who reach out to "take" something from me. I feel I must "carve out" my identity by "making my own way in the world."

These assumptions are axiomatic in a culture of death. Yet, they can also be recognized for the clichéd slogans they are once we realize they have nothing of God in them. In the Trinitarian Life of Divine *Communio*, Father, Son, and Holy Spirit do not experience love and freedom as antithetical. Their communion and their otherness are *mutually perfecting* and perfectly fulfilling of each other. Their relationship assumes and enhances the freedom and distinctiveness of each of the divine Persons. Difference is never division within the Trinity. Separateness is never separation. The "distance between" the Persons of the Trinity and their "intimacy with" Each Other obtain in direct, not inverse, proportion. What is sometimes a zero-sum game for us is a mystical ecstasy of complementarity for Father, Son, and Holy Spirit.[23]

We use the term "ecstasy" purposefully here. It properly refers to the nature of relationality among the Persons of the Trinity for two distinct reasons. First, because the word ecstasy derives from the Greek term, *"ek-stasis"*: a movement away from isolation and towards communion. God's very Personhood is *ex-static*. God is a *Communio* of three distinct Persons who "ex-ist" only *for, in, and towards* each other. If God were a *single* God, as the deists and general theists would have us believe, He would have to accept His ontological necessity and lose His inner freedom. But, as the Triune God who exists *only* as a loving relation among three distinct *Hypostases*, His very personhood is inherently *ek-static*. That is to say, each of the Persons of the Trinity exists only *for, in, and towards* the others. As Persons they "naturally seek" communion with the other. This "seeking of communion" is what actually "defines" their "nature" as God.

The *ek-stasis* of the Persons of the Trinity is also "ecstatic" in a divinely "erotic" sense. That is, the ecstatic mystery of loving intercourse, experienced at the human level in nuptial union and the marital act, is both and intimation and iconic image of the ecstatic intimacy that obtains among the Trinitarian Persons. More properly we should say, the human experience of ecstasy-in-communion in its many-splendored forms, is a reflection of, and participation in, the *ex-stasis* of the immanent Trinity.

*Perichoresis* is a term, coined by the church fathers, that also describes, in its own, untranslatable way, the *ecstatic communion* shared

---

[23] For a brilliant discussion of how "distance" and "intimacy" are perfectly reconciled and mutually enhancing within the divine *Communio Personarum*, see Hans Urs von Balthasar, *Theo-Drama: Theological Dramatic Theory, Volume V: The Last Act*, trans. Graham Harrison (San Francisco: Ignatius Press) 93-95. See also the person and book von Balthasar credits for his insights on this issue, Adrienne Von Speyr, *The World of Prayer*, 66, 210.

and circulated among the Persons of the Trinity. *Perichoresis* means "to contain" or "to penetrate." It refers to the three Persons of the Trinity as mutually "indwelling," or "permeating" each other. It intimates a joy, love, and *mutual interpenetration* (cf. John 17:10, 22-23) that is ineffable and indescribable. It attempts to convey how each of the Persons of the Trinity both wholly envelops and is wholly enveloped by the others. A "*perichoretic* sense" must characterize everything we contemplate about the workings of the Trinity. The mystery of *perichoresis* forms the basis of all forms of human communion that stem from and share in the life of the Trinity.

*Perichoresis* also connotes "to dance around." The Trinitarian Persons relate to each other by mutually indwelling, permeating, and interpenetrating, yet after the fashion of dancers whose communication and coordination enhance without infringing upon their separateness and otherness as they move together. "Infinite distance" and "unspeakable intimacy" are perfectly united in the life of the Trinity in a dynamic exceeding our capacity to conceive of. In Latin the equivalent term for *perichoresis* is *circumincession* ("moving around") or *circuminsessio* ("sitting around"). These terms also seek to convey a sense of closeness and reciprocity, intimacy and otherness, symbiosis and separateness, within the Trinity existing in a synergy of perfect harmony.

In addition to perichoresis and circumincession, there is one final foreign term that, properly understood, that can help us contemplate the *ek-static* nature of the Trinitarian Persons. I mentioned earlier that the Cappadocian Fathers, by distinguishing the concept of person (*hypostasis*) from substance (*ousia*), gave it a revolutionary, new meaning. This meaning was enhanced when they linked the term *hypostasis* (person) to the term "*prosopon*" (face). To be a person is to have a face. Human persons are created to "face" each other. They are intended to have "face-to-face" encounters. To be fully human is to "face" oneself and others in the same way as Father, Son, and Holy Spirit "face" each other in the Trinitarian *Communio*. When applied to the inner life of the Trinity, the term *prosopon* is more appropriately applied as a verb than a noun. For what is essential and ineffable for God is derivative and archetypal for human persons. The Persons of the Trinity "face" each other in their essential nature as divine Persons. Only the Incarnate Word, Jesus, has a human "face." Hence, it can be truly said that Jesus is "the human face of God."[24]

In Greek, *prosopon* consists of two words: *"pro"* ("for" or "towards") and *"opos"* ("optic" or "eye"). To be a *pros-opon* (person), therefore, means "to be-towards-a-face." It means to stand "in front of another's face." It means to be present to another within his or her field of vision. To speak about God as a *Communio* of Persons makes sense, therefore, only if we say God is, by nature, a communion of Persons who "face" each other. Each of the Persons of the Trinity ex-ists *for* and *towards* the other. Their very being *is* their *"facing"* of each other. To be a *Prosopon* (*Hypostasis*, Person) within the Trinity means intrinsically and ontological to "face" (to be "in front of," and "turned towards") the other. Like the term, *Hypostasis* (person), *Prosopon* indicates the reciprocally-enriching movement within God that defines the *ousia* (nature) of the Trinitarian Persons. It reveals God's *ex-sistence* as perpetual *ek-stasis* of Persons-in-communion.

Here we come to the heart of Trinitarian communion. The "turning towards" or "facing" of the *Prosopoi* of the Trinity is not merely external. The "being for" each other of Father, Son, and Holy Spirit, goes deeper than simply "being oriented" toward each other. It defines their "nature." It constitutes their "being." Among the Persons of the Trinity there obtains a union of indescribable *interpenetration and mutual participation*. Theirs is an ecstatic relationship of *co-inherence*. Each of the Persons in the Trinity "co-inheres" in the other. Each of the Persons of the Trinity "participates" in the other. Each of the Persons of the Trinity "interpenetrates" the other. Each of the Persons of the Trinity "indwells" the other. In each of the Persons in the Trinitarian *Communio*, therefore, we behold the mystery of infinite self-possession and total self-gift. And all of this without for a moment, or in the slightest degree, impinging upon the distinct integrity and ontological otherness of Father, Son, and Holy Spirit.

---

[24] See Christoph Schonborn, *God's Human Face: The Christ-Icon* (San Francisco: Ignatius Press, 1994).

It is beyond the capacity of our fallen intellect to grasp or properly appreciate the non-competitive co-inherence of the Trinitarian Persons.[25] The Fathers of the Church employed various images and analogies in their attempts to convey this mystery of mutual participation and intimate interpenetration.[26] A common metaphor for the mystery of *perichoretic* co-inherence, used by St. Athanasius and others, compared God the Father to a *Source* of Light, God the Son to a *Ray* of Light, and God the Holy Spirit to the Illumination, Radiance, and *Warmth* proceeding from the Light. Hillary of Poitiers described the unity-in-difference among the Trinitarian Persons as "...three suns cleaving to each other and giving out light, mingled and conjoined into one." Others imaged the Trinity as "Wellspring, Fountain, and Hydration" or "Root, Flower, Scent." No single image can do full justice to the Mystery of the Trinitarian *perichoresis*. All of these metaphors of Trinitarian mutuality attempt the impossible. They try to describe a relationship of co-inherence and mutual interpenetration which not only does not threaten the uniqueness of the Trinitarian *Hypostases*, but actually "strengthens" and "enriches" the respective singularity of Father, Son, and Holy Spirit.

This, then, is the fundamental Mystery of our Faith: The Trinity is a "Hypostatic Union" of three *inseparable but unconfused* divine Persons, whose perfect synergy of love and freedom, communion and otherness establish the primal form for all other mysteries. Not only are the human and divine natures "unmixed but undivided" in the Person of Jesus Christ, but the separate Persons of the Father, Son, and Holy Spirit also enjoy the same perichoretic, co-inherent relationship that we ascribe to the miracle of the Incarnation. This is a crucial point. From this perspective, the "hypostatic union" refers not simply to the union of the divine and human natures in Christ. It refers *more fundamentally* to

---

[25] Two splendid attempts to do justice to "non-competitive co-inherence" are Robert Barron, *The Priority of Christ* (Grand Rapids, MI: Brazos Press, 2007) and Kathryn Tanner, *Jesus, Humanity and the Trinity: A Brief Systematic Theology* (Minneapolis, MN: Fortress Press, 2001).

[26] For a fine summary of the patristic images of Trinitarian co-inherence, see David S. Cunningham, *The These Three Are One: The Practice of Trinitarian Theology* (Oxford: Blackwell Publishers Inc, 1998) 114, 180.

the being-as-communion within the Life of the Trinity itself. The *ousia* (nature) of Father, Son, and Holy Spirit is identical with their *perichoresis*. The essence of their Trinitarian Life is synonymous with their mutually-enriching and other-affirming interpenetration. Within the Life of the Trinity *unity differentiates*. The Trinitarian Persons are forever *indissolubly united but absolutely unmixed*. They enter into and envelop each other without the slightest compromise of their respective identities.

This fontal mystery of *perichoretic* coinherence within the Trinity is the indescribable taproot of all mysteries Christian. As we enter more deeply into our contemplation of the paradox of union and distinctiveness among the Persons of the Trinity, we begin to realize how God is a communion of personally distinct "Who's," never an amorphous, undifferentiated "What." We begin to see more clearly how God's existence does not precede His interpersonal communion as Father, Son, and Spirit. We begin to glimpse how God is always and forever a Communion of Persons, each surrendered to, and receiving of, the others.

We are now far removed from the fallen philosophical notion of a "Divine Substance" underlying, standing behind, or constituting the "Who" of Father, the Son, and the Holy Spirit. There is an "infinite distance" between the Persons within the Trinity, even while their union from all eternity is undivided and indivisible. "[W]e must not see this 'distance' in opposition to, or in conflict with, the 'closeness' (of circumincession in the one divine nature)…[for] such distance is necessary, for two reasons: first, in order to hold fast to the personal distinctness of each Person…and second, in order to establish the basis within the Trinity for what, in the economic Trinity, will be the possibility of a distance that goes as far as the Son's abandonment on the Cross."[27] Love within the Life of the Trinity, in other words, is a true exchange of Persons. It never resembles, in any way, a blending or homogenization of beings. The mystery of Jesus, as well as the truth of human persons, finds its illuminative source in the perichoretic unity-in-difference that defines and constitutes the life of the Trinity.

---

[27] Von Balthasar, *Theo-Drama, Volume. V* (hereafter TD, V): *The Last Act*, trans. Graham Harrison (San Francisco: Ignatius Press, 1998) 94.

*Section Two*

# Incarnation

# THE PRIORITY OF CHRIST[28]

*J*esus Christ is no ordinary man. He is the God-man: true God and true man. He is not a human person. Many Christians are astounded at this statement. Jesus is a human being but not a human person. He is a divine Person who assumed a human nature, and this for the purpose of His mission: the salvation of the world. Understanding these distinctions – forged with great passion and no little suffering in the early Councils of the Christian Church - brings us swiftly into the Mystery of the Incarnation.

"I am the Way, the Truth, and the Life. No one comes to the Father except through Me" (Jn. 14:6). "I and the Father are one" (Jn. 10:30). "Eternal life is this: to know You, the only true God, and Jesus Christ whom He has sent" (Jn. 17:3). Such audacious and ostensibly self-serving claims as these are either egocentric madness or, as C. Lewis pointed out, the truth. And, if they are the truth, then they change absolutely everything, including our ways of knowing and relating to God. They also fundamental alter our understanding of and disposition towards other human persons.

Jesus is both the Revelation and Incarnation of God. "The Word became flesh and dwelt among us" (Jn. 1:14). Here the evangelist John uses mystical language to convey what Karl Rahner asserted in theological terms: "the economic Trinity is the immanent Trinity."[29]

---

[28] The title of this section borrowed from Fr. Robert Barron's very fine book, *The Priority of Christ: Towards a Postliberal Catholicism* (Grand Rapids, MI: Brazos Press, 2007). Several of his insights inform the discussion here.

[29] Sometimes called "Rahner's Rule," this much commented-upon phrase first appeared in Karl Rahner, *The Trinity*, trans. Joseph Donceel (New York: Crossroad, 1997) 22.

What Rahner meant is: in and through the Person of Jesus of Nazareth, the Eternal Word made flesh, we truly encounter the fullness of the Trinity. The economic Trinity reveals and conveys the immanent Trinity, and the immanent Trinity is the Source and Cause of the economic Trinity.

The Eternal Word comes in the flesh to unite humanity with Himself. His purpose in so doing is to re-connect fallen human persons with His Father and their Holy Spirit. His mission is one of healing, reconciliation, and recapitulation. The word "salvation" does not do full justice to all that Jesus was born into the world to accomplish. He comes into the world to fully restore the cosmos to its original, lost unity. He comes to fulfill what St. Paul calls, "…the Mystery of His Will…which He set forth in Christ as a Plan for the fullness of time, to unite all things in Himself, things in heaven and on earth" (Eph. 1:9-10).

Christ is the Alpha the Omega, the Beginning and the End (Rev. 1:8). In Him all things have their beginning, purpose, and end. He is the Source and Summit of everything and everyone that exists. Everything that is created is made with an eye to the only Son of God. The Father "sees and loves in us, what He sees and loves in Christ."[30] The Father's infinite love of us is ultimately a function of His eternal and unconditional love of His Son, in whose image and likeness we are made. As the Second Person of the Trinity come among us, Jesus of Nazareth, the Christ (Messiah) of God, is the Keystone of history. He is the Eternal Word who "makes all things new" (Rev. 21:5).

It is important not to underestimate the gravity of what is being asserted here. The ontological priority of Christ affects and determines how we know and relate to Him and to everything else the world. We cannot know Jesus as we might believe we know another person or any other thing. Neither Divine nor human persons are "things," and even our knowledge of earthly things is radically altered in light of how we acquire knowledge of Jesus.

How is it that we know things truly only in the light of Christ? "I am

---

[30] Prefaces for Sundays in Ordinary Time VII, Roman Rite.

the Light of the world," claims Jesus,"...those who follow me will not walk in darkness but have the light of life" (Jn. 8:12). "In Your light, O Lord, we see light" (Ps. 36:9). We recall from our earlier discussion that only a "hermeneutic of love or loyalty" enables us to receive dimensions of Divine Truth otherwise inaccessible to scientific, objective human knowing. Knowing Christ Jesus intensifies this mystery. Knowledge of Christ is "participation" (*methexis*) in Christ. It is mystically coming to share in the very nature of Christ as both man and God. It is also to share in His knowledge and intimacy with the Father and their Holy Spirit. Knowledge of Jesus, in other words, is *participation in the Life and knowledge of the Trinity Itself.* It is our incorporation into the *Communio Personarum* of the Trinity. It totally transforms and transfigures the mind, bodies, and hearts of those who come to enjoy it.

Any analysis of Christ from the perspective other than that of someone who has entered mystically into the divine Person of Jesus is fundamentally flawed, regardless how 'critical,' 'historical,' or 'scientifically accurate' it pretends to be. The whole history of philosophy and theology, since at least the 14th century, has tended to put the philosophical cart in front of the theological horse when trying to understand the nature and Person of Jesus. "Faith seeking understanding (*Fides quaerens intellectum*)" has gradually become "reason proving faith" or "faith needing to justify itself in the court of reason." The contemplative connection has been broken. A rift has been opened between faith and understanding, between dogmatic and practical theology.

Hans Urs von Balthasar was deeply concerned about what he described as the "fatal cleavage" between theology from spirituality in contemporary Christianity. He believed this fatal separation constituted the greatest tragedy in the history of theology.[31] What had been seamless

---

[31] See especially his famous essay, "Theology and Sanctity," in *Explorations in Theology, Volume I* (hereafter ET, I): The Word Made Flesh  (San Francisco: Ignatius Press, 1989), 181-213. See also: Von Balthasar, "The Unity of Theology and Spirituality," in *Convergences: To the Source of Christian Mystery*, trans. E.A. Nelson (San Francisco: Ignatius Press, 1983), and "Theology and Holiness," *Communio: International Catholic Review* 16 (Fall, 1989) 351-65.

in the patristic tradition – the unity of theology and spirituality – has been torn apart. A thousand different false dichotomies have resulted from the divorce of dogmatic and mystical theology. This, in turn, has led to the confusion and spiritual detriment of the faithful. A more prayerful, mystical, and contemplative approach to the Person of Jesus is Christ is called for if the Mystery of our Redemption is once again to be apprehended and appreciated in all its *kenotic* glory. [32]

In this regard, Jean-Luc Marion, a devout and eminent Catholic post-modern philosopher has stressed an important difference between *Theo*logy and theo*logy*. *Theo*logy [called by some "**theo**-ontology"] insists that all knowledge and language about God is *determined by God's own logic*. It begins and ends with what the Trinity has disclosed about God's *perichoretic* inner Life. The inner life of the Trinity is on display in iconic form in the Incarnation. Jesus is the enfleshed hologram of the Triune *Communio Personarum*. We have no other real knowledge of God other than that which Jesus affords us *in His very own Person*. It is not primarily the words or teaching of Jesus that comprise Revelation, it is his entire Person. Every one of Jesus' words, deeds, actions, and associations is a theophany or epiphany of Trinitarian Love.

The alternative way of thinking about Jesus is what Marion calls theo*logy* [sometimes called "**onto**-theology"]. Theo*logy* insists that Jesus can and must be understood just like any other phenomenon of history, i.e., through the use of critical reason, and by subjecting the historical Jesus to the canons of scientific inquiry and disinterested historical research. The so-called "Quest for the historical Jesus" is one such attempt to grasp the Lord according to the categories of fallen human understanding. In this endeavor, Jesus is "interpreted" according to the least common rationalistic denominators. Instead of being seen as the determiner and creator of human reason and the Source of "the renewal of our minds" (Eph. 4:23), Jesus is viewed as a function of a prior, more primordial criteria of truth. Instead of being seen as "The Way, the Truth, and the Life (Jn. 14:6)," He is approached as an example or instance of a more fundamental way,

---

[32] *Kenotic* means "self-emptying" or (better) "self-dispossessing."

truth, or life. Balthasar calls this quest for a higher experience of God or truth other than the Incarnation "the primal lie."[33] Like Balthasar, Marion is prescient in his insistence that everything is at stake in deciding whether Jesus precedes and overshadows being or whether being precedes God, and can therefore be adequately and accurately grasped apart from illumination in Him Who calls Himself "Light of the world" (Jn. 8:12).

In opting for what Marion calls *theo*-logy, we make common cause with the saints of the Catholic tradition who, like Augustine and Aquinas, believe that not only did Christ create everything that is "All things were made through Him, and without Him nothing was made that was made" (Jn. 1:3), but nothing is known other that what can be known "in Him." "In Him was life, and the life was the light of men," says St. John (Jn. 1:4). To say that Jesus is "the Light of the world" (Jn. 8:12) is no mere metaphor. It is *in Christ and through Christ* that even the simplest act of knowing takes place. Human understanding is thoroughly Christological, indeed Trinitarian, even at its most fundamentally "natural" level. These are metaphysical, indeed mystical assertions, upon which depend the entire edifice of human understanding and ultimate well-being. We can ill afford to get the equation wrong if we wish "all men to be saved and come to knowledge of the truth" (1 Tim. 2:4).

Just as it takes a special grace to conceive at the Trinity as a Community of Divine Persons (*Communio Personarum*), it takes another actual grace to conceive of truth as incarnate in the Person of Jesus. We don't readily imagine "truth" as a Person. We have as "substantialist" a notion of truth as we have of God. It seems almost second nature for us to conceive of "being" as ontologically preceding the Eternal Word and His Incarnation. Our mental "default" position is to sub-consciously imagine Jesus as "fitting into" the categories of natural and scientific reason. As a man he was obviously a historical person,

---

[33] *The Glory of the Lord: A Theological Aesthetics, volume 2, Studies in Theological Style: Clerical Styles*, trans. Andrew Louth, John Saward, Martin Simon, Rowan Williams, Francis McDonagh and Brian McNeil (San Fancisco: Ignatius Press, 1984) 66.

subject to the laws of nature and patterns and paradoxes of history. It therefore seems quite "natural" to seek to grasp the greatness of Jesus in terms familiar to our normal ways of knowing and understanding. But this is a mistake. Jesus is first and foremost a Divine Person. He entered human history as a man, but He is always the God-man who forever *transcends* history. As God, He contains all of history within Himself. He is the center and key to history. Everything is created by, and oriented to, Who He Is. Like the disciples on the road to Emmaus, we fail to apprehend the real Jesus if we conceive of him only in human terms. Though they were seeing the "man" who was speaking to them on the road, they did not recognize Him as Jesus until they received the special illumination of the Holy Spirit. Then, "their eyes were opened" (Lk.24:31). They realized, with "burning hearts" (Lk. 24:32) that "Jesus is Lord." So too for us. It takes a special grace, and a mental and spiritual *metanoia* (conversion), to realize that by "coming into the world," Jesus, is "the true light which enlightens ever person" (Jn 1:9). It is the pride, envy, and every other deadly sin, combined with the evil influences of the "powers and principalities" (Eph. 6:12), that render us as dull and difficult as the original disciples in discerning the divine Person of Jesus as "the Way, the Truth, and the Life" (Jn. 14:6). As a function of that same pride, rebellion, and insolence, it is easily to pay lip service to these clichés of our faith without interiorizing them unto a total renewal of our minds and hearts.

# THE GREAT DIVORCE

*A* wasteland of modern the*ology* has resulted from trying to define Jesus in terms of human knowing. Instead of allowing our minds and hearts to be transfigured by the Light of Christ, we have attempted to cram the Mystery of Christ into the categories of our own flawed understanding. Long gone are the days of the early and medieval Church where the patristic observation rang true: "If you are a theologian you will pray truly; and if you pray truly you are a theologian."[34] Gone too are the days when the only theologians were the saints. For centuries we have suffered a separation of critical reason from the light of faith. For far too long we have had to endure the effects of the divorce of theology from a contemplative and mystical Catholic spirituality.

One tragic effect of the great divorce of theology from sanctity is that God, Jesus, and His Mystical Body, the Church, have been *objectified*. These divine Mysteries are now thought to belong to the same basic metaphysical category, to share the same genus of being, as other objects in the world. We noted above how this same insidious equivalence can infect even intensely pious and apparently orthodox Catholic thinking. We might call this infection the "heresy of univocity." To treat God and "being" as univocal means to speak about them as if they are terms of equal weight within a common frame of reference. Often, in this framework, God is imagined to be *larger* than the world but not of a fundamentally different order. His "transcendence" is imagined to consist is something larger, but not completely "other," than all of which He has created. The doctrine of creation *ex nihilo* is not grasped

---

[34] Evagrius, *On Prayer*, #61.

in such a framework in all its arresting, revolutionary significance. This leads inexorably to various sorts of pantheism, monism, panentheism, and other essentially intra-mundane ways of imagining God and Jesus as macro-versions of something natural or human.

Theology deteriorates into glorified anthropology whenever, tacitly or explicitly, there is presumed to be no *qualitative* difference between Christ and the creatures He has made. Whenever Jesus and human persons are thought to be the same order of things, Christianity becomes merely a "religion." It ceases to be the transforming *kerygma* that turned the Roman Empire upside down. It ceases to be a manifestation of the Holy Spirit, gathering all persons and creation into the 2nd Adam, Jesus Christ. The Trinity must be conceived of as ontologically "other" than the things of creaton, Otherwise an insidious univocity is at work which, if left unchallenged, destroys *theo*-logy defined as "faith seeking understanding."

Here is where orthodox Trinitarian Christianity draws the line. God is **not** a Being "of the same kind" as other being(s). Some beings, especially human beings, are created in the "image and likeness of God" (*imago Dei*). Because of this, they may be conceived of as *analogous to God.* Yet, God must be exclusively affirmed as the primary analogue in any comparison between Himself and human persons. There is all the difference in the world between saying man is made in the image and likeness of God (Gen. 1:26) and that God exists in the "image and likeness of man" (Feuerbach).

Whereas the patristic and contemplative scholastic *theo*logians held – like the prophets of the Old Testament and the saints and mystics of the New Dispensation – that the Triune God is categorizable in no genus or substantive conception whatsoever, lesser theo*logians* insist that both God and man can and must be understood in logical categories that somehow precede and include God and man as objects. When this occurs, theology and philosophy separate, and the priority of Revelation is lost amidst an ever-accelerating descent into *onto*-theology.

Historically, *onto*-theology has taken very predictable forms. From the monism, pantheism or syncretism of the ancient and pre-Christian philosophies such as Buddhism and Hinduism, to the elaborate and systematic idealism of Hegel and Marx, the priority of Christ is replaced by the forms, categories, and underlying assumptions of a pre-existing religious or intellectual framework. Instead of being grasped at the point where it is incarnate and made manifest – in Jesus Christ, the Alpha and Omega (Rev. 1:8) – truth is said to be found elsewhere: under, over, behind, or around the Person of Jesus of Nazareth. His contact with history in the Incarnation is thought to divest Him of His divine prerogative to *establish* the categories of knowing. He is said to be known by us, not us by Him. Yet, it is in Him that "we live, and move, and have our being" (Acts 17:28). Overlooking this fundamental fact of Revelation, everything else becomes feeling our way in the dark, mistaking the chimera of human opinion for the translucent light of truth that flows from the Person of Jesus Christ.

Some movements of modern theo-*logy* have sought to re-interpret Jesus in terms of a prior agenda or the canons of an alternate truth, such as the demythologizing of Rudolph Bultmann, the Quest for the Historical Jesus of the Jesus Seminar, or the Creation Theology of Matthew Fox. For these fashionable theorists, Jesus is not the Truth Incarnate. He is *an example* of some truth they have identified as existing prior to Christ. *They* have established the criteria to which Jesus must be compared and judged. This is simply projection posturing as insight. In truth, Jesus IS the Truth. "I am the Way, the Truth, and the Life," He says, "no one comes to the Father except through me" (Jn. 14:6). Until this "truth" is understood as being the very Person of Jesus, everything else pretending to be true about Jesus is patently false. There is no true knowledge "about" Jesus until there is knowledge "of" Jesus (spiritual, intimate, mystical, and contemplative). Only those who have entered mystically into the divine Person of Jesus can speak with authority about "Who" vs. "what" Jesus is and means.

Imagining "something prior" to Jesus Christ, then, is the death of the spiritual life. Since *theo*logy and spirituality are identical in the patristic and contemplative tradition, approaching Jesus apart from prayer and adoration is a mistake. We must approach Him on our knees if we are to grasp Him in his proper glory as God. Like Mary of Bethany (Lk. 10:39-42), we must sit frequently and contemplatively at the Master's feet if we are to hear His creative Word. It is nothing less than insolence when a theo*logian* makes a claim to be able to subject the Christ to extrinsic measures. It is equally irreverent when a modern day Gnostic attempts to explain away the uniqueness of Christ by reducing the Mystery of His Person to categories of general sensibility.

The splendor of truth and the glory of the Lord are obscured when Jesus is scrutinized by the categories of historical analysis or placed presumptively beneath the microscope of so-called scientific inquiry. This is particularly evident in the widespread reductionist use of the so-called historical-critical method of biblical interpretation. As Pope Benedict XVI has said repeatedly: despite the helpfulness and appropriateness of the historical-critical method in the study of Scripture, this methodology becomes an instrument of atheism when it functions as an ideology. "According to this hermeneutic [of suspicion], when there seems to be a divine element [that Jesus interjects into history], one must explain where it came from and [attempt to reduce] it to the human element completely. Because of this, interpretations that deny the historicity of divine elements emerge."[35] It is, of course, precisely the Divine Personhood of the God-man that the purveyors of onto-theo*logy* are seeking to deny.

Enough has been said to illustrate the corrosive and exceedingly misleading ideology of those who prefer a measure of truth prior to that of Christ. Sad to say, the theological atmosphere of the modern Church is contaminated with cross-currents of this noxious methodology. Its grip on even pious minds is so very deep because its tacit assumptions are cleverly hidden and disguised. Where one has not had the benefit of a strongly evangelical and/or contemplative formation, it is virtually inevitable that such theo*logical* claptrap will have a natural appeal. The antidote to this humanistic exegesis must avoid what Pope Benedict XVI calls the false alternatives of "pious pelagiansim" and a "sclerotic

---

[35] Address to Bishop's Synod, 10/14/08. For a superb treatment of Benedict XVI's assessment of historical-critical method, see Scott Hahn, *Covenant and Communion: The Biblical Theology of Pope Benedict XVI* (Grand Rapids, MI: Brazos Press, 2009) esp. 25-63.

neo-scholasticism."[36] Instead, it must be based solidly on a revival of the mystical and patristic roots of our contemplative Catholic tradition.

It is a matter of sadness and grief to see the glory of the Eternal Word regarded as a "symbol" of a more "archetypal truth" or "necessary principle." It is a crucifixion for the people of God to watch theo*logians* reduce the Divine Logos to an expression of general religious consciousness, or to a validation of some moral or aesthetic principle. It is a ***theo***-logical purgatory to watch the historical-critical method used as a cudgel to hammer the Mystery of God-Incarnate into the narrow categories of an agenda-driven framework. All the theo-***logical*** personages who engage in this nefarious enterprise have one thing in common: the fear of allowing Jesus to reveal the glory of His Face, disarming them of their theological systems, and confronting them with the challenge of conversion. They seek to *use* the Person of Christ to substantiate their own pre-existing schemes, rather than bending the knee to Him in faith and surrendering in obedience to His unconditional Will. They lack the courage to allow Him, God's Creative Word, to reconfigure their intellects and realign their priorities. Nothing is more deleterious to the true **theo**-logical task than constructing a theological framework into which the Trinity is supposedly to fit. Theological systems, as Balthasar cautioned, are the death of all true Christology.[37] Never has this been as true as in this era of post-Enlightenment ***onto***-theo***logy***.

Let us return to a more contemplative Christology. Let us pursue a more mystical Christology that re-unites **theo**-logy and prayer. "Theology at prayer," as experienced in the early Church, has been replaced by "theology at the desk." We need a reunion of theology

---

[36] Joseph Cardinal Ratzinger, *The Yes of Jesus Christ* (New York: The Crossroad Publishing Company, 1991) 82. For a larger discussion of Pope Benedict XVI's attempt to elevate our vision of Christianity as a mystery that goes far beyond mere moralism, see Tracey Rowland, *Ratzinger's Faith: The Theology of Pope Benedict XVI* (Oxford: Oxford University Press, 2008) 66-83.

[37] "Nothing is so much the stigma of a mediocre spirit as the drive and enthusiasm for the systematization of ultimate things." See Hans Urs von Balthasar, *The Grain of Wheat: Aphorisms* (San Francisco: Ignatius Press, 1995) 21ff.

and sanctity. Knowledge of Jesus can no more be separated from an attitude of prayer than *gnosis* can replace faith as the bedrock of Christian life. God and Jesus are "ever-greater (*Ja mehr*)." The Mystery of the Incarnation is appreciated as if for the very first time when the being of God is seen to transcend all categories of human thought. "In Your Light we see light, O Lord" (Ps. 36:9). Only when we see God as "totally other" - yet as the One, Who in His great love for us, has come among us as a man — will the patristic ideal of "Faith seeking understanding" once again be realized.

# GOD WITHOUT BEING:
# A MYSTICAL CHRISTOLOGY

*I*ronically, it is a group of philosophers known as "post-modernist" who can help facilitate the *ressourcement* ("return to the sources") that Pope Benedict XVI and others insist is the key to the New Evangelization. One such thinker is Jean-Luc Marion, the Catholic philosopher, whose distinction, mentioned above, between **theo**logy and theo**logy**, illustrates the fundamental difference between thinking and speaking about God in ways driven by God's own Revelation, versus a more reductionist approach that subjects the divine Mystery to prefabricated categories of human understanding. In this approach, Marion agrees with Aquinas. The "being" of God is that Mystery *through which* all creation exists; yet, God Himself is not *part of* that creation. Marion thus continues the venerable Catholic tradition that refuses to conceive of "God" as a "Being" equivalent to, univocal with, or in any way in the same category (genus) as other Being or beings that God has made.

To solidify this important Catholic point, Marion says it is best to describe God as "God without Being."[38] Despite the ambiguity of this phrase, Marion's elliptical language reminds us that the "otherness" of God – and therefore of Jesus – must strongly inform our reflections on the Trinity and the Incarnation. God is never just another being alongside all the other beings in the universe. Nor is God ever simply "Being-writ-large." God is not in competition with the world, nor is He comparable to the world within any frames of reference that can be drawn from the world. God is neither one being among many, nor the

---

[38] J-L Marion, *God Without Being.*

43

totality of all beings taken together. No form of pantheism or monism can account for the Mystery of God. God transcends, yet inheres in, the world He created, but in a manner that can be best apprehended only "in Christ." These crucial distinctions can be grasped and understood only through mystical and contemplative intimacy with Jesus in prayer.

What many post-modern theologians reclaim through their appreciation of God's "total otherness" (alterity), they sometimes forfeit through their agendas of theo*logical* abstraction. We turn our attention, therefore, to two *theo*logians who, though thoroughly "modern," have no other agenda than that of Jesus Christ, namely the Catholic, Hans Urs von Balthasar and the Protestant, Karl Barth. These two great men had a close and enduring friendship. They shared a love of Mozart, as well a transformative relationship with many of the great saints of the Church. Most of all they shared a deep love for the Person of Jesus Christ. Their common "hermeneutic of love" made possible a great friendship and communion between them, despite their on-going theological differences. Rather than analyze these differences, I will focus on what they have in common, and what I believe to be their common genius in strengthening our appreciation of the Word-become-flesh.

Balthasar saw in Barth's *theo*logy much of the same beauty he was attempting to convey in his own. This Beauty, of course, is the Face of Jesus Christ. Barth broke with the demythologizers of his day and with the **onto**-theo**logians** of the 1930's when he saw how a Christianity that subjected Christ to the agendas of historians and philosophers enabled a Nazi regime to perpetuate evil. From that time on, Barth recognized the futility of attempting to deal with God without kneeling before Him in a spirit of love, hope, and contrition. Karl Barth saw the on-going need of allowing the Divine Word of God to judge and deliver, accuse and convert, according to His purposes and inscrutable Will.

For Barth, as for Balthasar, *theo*logy is truly **Theo**centric only when it is **Christo**centric. Barth developed his *"anolgia fidei"* ("analogy of faith") as a Protestant alternative to the Catholic *"analogia entis"* ("analogy of being"). According to Barth's *analogia fidei*, all knowledge of God rests upon *a prior revelation* of God from above. We *enter into* this knowledge of God by freely surrendering our own concepts of truth to the miracle of Revelation. We make a decision to allow our minds and hearts to be reconfigured, through faith, by adoring, worshipping, and praying to the Person of Jesus Christ. God's self-revelation can be grasped only at the point where it is most clearly expressed: at its center, in Jesus Christ, the Lord of Lords and the King of Kings.

This approach to **theo**logy is sometimes called 'positive' theology or 'evangelical' Christianity. Barth opposed this approach to what he called 'natural theology.' Evangelical theology, he insisted, begins and ends with an *encounter* with the *living Word of God*. The Truth is not a "something;" it is always and forever a Someone (Jesus). God is a God-of-relationship, a covenantal God. He is ineluctably relational within His own Life as Trinity. He is also relational in His elective relationships. He is a covenantal God. He establishes unbreakable bonds with His people He chooses to be His own. He is a inherently and ineluctably a God of *communio, koinonia,* and *sobornost.* He is a God of address and encounter. Knowing God in Christ, therefore, is always an *event.* It is never merely an academic exercise or an intellectual insight. God is "ever greater." He can never be captured or defined by any human categories or philosophical concepts. He is always "other than" and "greater than" that of which human beings can conceive.

It is no surprise that one of the most brilliant and devout theologians of the medieval tradition, St. Anselm, was a pivotal figure in Barth's own intellectual and spiritual conversion. St. Anselm formulates a "definition" of God which serves to show that God cannot be defined. It comes in the form of a prayer: "...we believe You to be that than which nothing greater can be thought," prays Anselm.[39] This is the equivalent of saying that whatever we can conceive of is, by definition, *less than and other than* God. Any concept of God, no matter how lofty, subtle, or transcendental, is always "overshadowed" our "outdistanced" by the *reality* of God.

To think we can think adequately of God is the epitome of *hubris* (pride) according to Barth. Even to think of God as "the unsurpassable"

---

[39] *Prosologion,* chapter 2.

is to assume a standpoint outside of God, which is impossible for the human person. It is also to presume to stand "above" God, somehow judging and categorizing God according to fallen, human notions. The Lord, insists Barth, mocks all such speculation. As Isaiah says, "As far as the heavens are above the earth, so high are my ways above your ways (Isa. 55:9)." Karl Barth credited St. Anselm with awakening his evangelical sense that the God of Abraham, Isaac, Jacob, and Jesus was ever more, never less, than the God of the philosophers, no matter how sophisticated or subtle such philosophers claimed to be.

Balthasar admired the Christocentric theology of Karl Barth and patterned some of his own Christological reflections after Barth's *Church Dogmatics*. Yet Balthasar took the Christology of Barth to mystical dimensions unreachable for the Calvinist who lacked a developed sense of the Catholic contemplative tradition. Mysticism, for Balthasar, is *a participation in* the living Person of Jesus Christ.[40] Like Karl Barth, Balthasar attempted to capture the "here and now" reality of the crucified and risen Christ. He sought to revive a sense that every meeting with Jesus Christ is an "event" and an "encounter." With Barth, Balthasar seeks to "actualize" the doctrine of the Incarnation. Far too often Jesus is understood as simply an historical personage, even by those who profess belief in His Resurrection. In truth, the Mystery of Christ envelops and transcends His Incarnation as Jesus of Nazareth. Christology, for Balthasar, can only be worthily undertaken by men and women who have "entered into" the *present Life* of Jesus Christ.

"Mystical," for Balthasar, refers to contact with the Trinity through an existential encounter with the risen Jesus. It is inseparably tied to the Incarnation and the Paschal Mystery. The last thing in the world "mystical" means is "metaphorical." "Mystical" means "more real" than the merely empirical. It is never less than meditation upon the historical

---

[40] Barth also has a "doctrine of participation," but it lacks the ontological dimensions conveyed by Balthasar's treatment, and tends to echo the "imputed" tones of much of evangelical Protestantism. See Adam Neder, *Participation in Christ: An Entry into Karl Barth's Church Dogmatics* (Louisville, KY: Westminster John Knox Press, 2009).

Jesus, but it is also always "more than" an intellectual or emotional experience. It is a real participation in the "ever more" of the Mystery of God. Only a genuinely "mystical" encounter with Christ enables us to overcome the separation of doctrine from practice, theology from spirituality. Because it is real contact with Christ, "mystical" *theo*logy is not a "subjective experience of glory and...stamped as an exception." It is, on the contrary, the avenue to and epitome of holiness to which all Christians are called.[41]

In this same vien, the dogmatic tradition of the Church must not be seen as mysticism's opposite, i.e., as "the strictly logical and intellectualist metaphysics of the Church."[42] Like Newman, Balthasar had a passion for rescuing dogma from the dustbin of neo-scholasticism and re-appropriating it according to the patristic and early monastic traditions. "Far from opposing each other," Balthasar says, "dogmatic and mystical theologies are, if one conceives of theology as a dynamic realization, even *identical*. It is thus that all the church fathers understand things, and most particularly Origen and the Cappadocians."[43]

Because "mystical," for Balthasar, means personally and intimately encountering Jesus Christ in and through every dogmatic and sacramental aspect of revealed truth, he repudiates any approach to Christology that would "look on historical revelation as a past event... and not as something always happening, to be listened to and obeyed."[44] "Mystical" means "being drawn into the here-and-now Person of Jesus Christ," including His Paschal Mystery. Mystical participation in Christ means being given a real share in the redemptive mission of the Messiah.

The concept of our "participation in Christ" is the key to unlocking the kind of mystical *theo*logical and Christological vision that Barth, Balthasar, and Benedict XVI seek to restore. "Participation" (*methexis*),

---

[41] See the Documents of Vatican II on the Universal Call to Holiness.

[42] *The Glory of the Lord: A Theological Aesthetic,* Volume V (hereafter GL, V), trans. Brian McNeil, C.R.V., Andrew Louth, John Saward, Rowan Williams, Oliver Davies (San Francisco: Ignatius Press, 1991) 26.

[43] Quoted by Mark A. McIntosh, *Christology From Within: Spirituality and the Incarnation in Hans Urs Von Balthasar* (Notre Dame, IN: Notre Dame Press, 2000) 13-14.

[44] Von Balthasar, ET, I, 205.

as the Church Fathers understood it, has a deeper, more "mystical," meaning that our modern use of this term implies. "Participation in Christ" means "coinherence" in Christ. It shares in and reflects the interpenetration of the Persons of the Trinity. It connotes an "assimilation" or "assumption" into Jesus' very own divine Person. Life "in Christ" is always more than simply the "imitation of Christ." It means "entering into Christ." It means encountering Jesus and enjoying intimate *communio* with Him. We can thank Marion, Barth, Balthasar, and Benedict XVI for reminding us that the living Person of Jesus is the Alpha and Omega, the term and the terminus, of all our knowledge of the Triune God.

*Section Three*

# Corpus Mysticum

# LIFE IN CHRIST

"*I* am the Alpha and the Omega," says Jesus, "the Beginning and the End" (Rev. 1:8). The Incarnation, as central as it is to the mystery of Christian faith, is not the end of the story. Jesus' Incarnation stands mid-way between the beginning and end of His identity and His mission as the Eternal Word.

There are two "comings" in the mystery of Christ, one at the midpoint of salvation history, and one at the end of God's mysterious Plan for creation (Eph. 1:10). "In the beginning was the Word. The Word was with God, and the Word was God" (Jn. 1:1). Jesus, the Eternal Word of God, pre-existed his advent as man in Jesus of Nazareth. His first coming, initiated by His assumption of our human nature in the womb of the Virgin Mary through the power of the Holy Spirit, results in His Incarnation. This first coming of the Eternal Word in the flesh is to be followed by His "coming again in glory." This takes place after "He has put all enemies under His feet" (1 Cor. 15:25; cf. Heb. 10:13). Christ, in other words, stands at the beginning of creation as the One "through whom all things were made" (Jn. 1:3), and at the end of history when all things are brought to completion in Him (cf. Eph. 1:21).

Between these two times, Christ actively gathers all nations unto Himself, that He might make of them an acceptable sacrifice to His Father. Even from His position seated at the right hand of the Father, Jesus is still at work "reconciling the world to Himself." "My Word does not proceed from me without doing the work for which I have sent it. Just as snow and rain do not fall upon the earth, water it, and return, nor does my Word come down without accomplishing the task for which I have sent it" (Isa. 55:11). Jesus' mission, indeed His "coming to full stature" (Eph. 4:13), is still mysteriously in progress. Through His Paschal Mystery He has already "accomplished all things;" yet, through the power of His Holy Spirit, the salvation He won is still in the process of "being brought to completion" (cf. Rom. 8:18-25).

A properly Trinitarian vision of Christ – a truly mystical, contemplative, patristic understanding of Christ – begins and ends with seeing Jesus as a Person whose identity is being-in-communion, both vertically and horizontally. In the Life of the Trinity, Jesus, as Son and Eternal Word, is never without the Father. Similarly, in His Incarnation, He is never without those He has chosen to be His *indispensable associates*. He has chosen, selected, and called others to be *participators, sharers, and co-redeemers* with Himself. The persons we associate most closely with Jesus historical mission as Redeemer – His Mother, His Apostles, and his disciples - are as ingredient to His identity as Savior as the Father and Spirit are essential to His *Hypostasis* as Son. So also with us. As members of His "Mystical Body," the Church, we are essentially bound up with, and engrafted into, His personal identity as Savior and God-man. Grasping the *gravitas* of such assertions requires, and results in, a deepening appreciation of the Person of Christ. It demands a contemplative vision that can apprehend the mystery of the Mystical Body of Christ (*Corpus Mysticum*).

"The Mystical Body of Christ" (*Corpus Mysticum*) is a term that describes the Mystery of Jesus as a Divine Person-in-communion. Yet, the term, "Mystical Body," must be rescued from centuries of misunderstanding and misappropriation. We live far downstream from the wellspring of the patristic tradition in which *Corpus Mysticum* was understood in ways opposite of the meaning we have often attached to the "Mystical Body of Christ." In a later section we will outline some important differences in greater detail. Here it is enough to enjoin a contemplative sense of Jesus as *Corpus Mysticum*. For this is how the Church Father understood Him: as a Mystical Person "reconciling all things in Himself" (2 Cor. 5:19). Saints such as Ignatius of Antioch, Irenaeus of Lyons, Gregory of Nyssa, and many others, viewed Jesus not simply or even primarily as a historical figure. They saw Him as a *Corporate Person*. For them, He is a Divine Person who *assumed a human nature* for the purpose of uniting and "recapitulating" (restoring, renewing) all things in Himself. The concepts of "Corporate Person," "assumption," and "assimilation of all things in Christ," are critical if we are to recapture the profound and pristine, mystical and contemplative, vision of our Fathers in the faith.

Perhaps an intermediate step to re-entering the mystical depths of the patristic tradition is to ponder for a moment the meaning of the simple, yet pivotal, phrase "in Christ" ("*en Christo*"). Used by St. Paul over 160 times in his epistles, the phrase "in Christ" denotes an intimacy with Christ that includes but transcends, completes and fulfills, our ordinary dealings with Him. What, exactly, does it mean to be "in Christ"? What does it mean to live "in Christ" or to "participate in Him"? What is involved in finding my identity "in Christ"? The answers to these questions will determine the depth and quality of our relationship with the Eternal Word.

We know from Scripture that Jesus often identifies Himself with certain human persons. "Saul, Saul, why are you persecuting Me" (Acts 9:4). "When you do it to the least of my brethren, you do it to Me" (Mt. 25:40). "He who hears you, hears me" (Lk Mt. 18:18). How are we to understand this identification of the Savior with those He is saving?

More than anyone before him, St. Paul grasped – in a mystical vision (Acts 9:1-9; 22:5-16; 26:10-18) – that Jesus is no mere historical figure. He knew in a moment's revelation that this Christ, whom he encountered on the road to Damascus, was both God and man. He instantly understood that Jesus is capable of incorporating all those "He had predestined before the foundation of the world" (Eph. 1:4-5) into His very divine Person. St. Paul knew upon his conversion that Christ is able to assimilate others into Himself in such a manner that their shared life can be ontologically described as "one." To live "in Christ," therefore, is the key phrase that unlocks the mystery of what has been aptly described as "Pauline Mysticism" (see Rom. 6:11; 8:1; 12:5; 16:3-10; 1 Cor. 2, 30; 4:10; 15:18; 2 Cor. 5:17; 12:2; Gal. 1:22; 2:4; 3:26; Col.

1:2, 4).[45] The mystical and contemplative vision of St. Paul, who sees the "total Christ" (*Christus Totus*) incorporating and recapitulating all things in Himself, must become our own if we are to fully appreciate the mystery of God-become-man in Jesus.

One of the reasons St. Paul is said to be so notoriously difficult to understand is because his mystical concept of living "in Christ" is not sufficiently grasped. St. Paul is speaking of a "knowledge" of Jesus Christ that extends far beyond our usual definitions of knowledge. St. Paul is trading upon a biblical understanding of "knowledge." To "know" another person, biblically speaking, is to have intimate, often carnal, "knowledge" of them (Gen. 4:1). St. Paul is calling us from an "extrinsic," "forensic," and "transactional" relationship with Christ to a more biblical, intimate, and ultimately "mystical," "knowledge" of Him. St. Paul envisions a form of "nuptial" or "intercoursal" knowledge of Jesus that derives from, and participates in, the mysterious intimacy of the Trinity itself. To live "in Christ," therefore, is to "partake of" or "participate in" Jesus in such a way that we are *incorporated into* His own ecstatic intimacy with the Father and the Holy Spirit.

We return again to the relations among the Trinitarian Persons in order to grasp the reality of becoming one with Christ. Christianity, in our time, has been reduced to a two-dimensional, flat, utilitarian distortion of the unfathomable depths of the Trinitarian and Incarnational Mystery. For centuries now, the "imitation of Christ" has passed as an acceptable, indeed admirable, substitute for "participation in Christ." "Following Jesus" has been thought, mistakenly, to exhaust the meaning of "being a believer." But "being a believer," from a "participatory" view, means to be so "initiated into Christ" that we

---

[45] Pauline Mysticism is a theme championed mostly by great Catholic exegetes in the past, though popularized by the agnostic Albert Schweitzer (*The Mysticism of Paul the Apostle*, 1931), and making a comeback today even among evangelical Protestants (see James D. G. Dunn, *The Theology of Paul the Apostle* (Grand Rapids, MI: William B. Eerdmans Publishing Company, 1998), 390-410). For an excellent contemporary Catholic description and evaluation of the history and current status of the debate regarding Pauline Mysticism, see Romano Penna, *Paul the Apostle: Wisdom and Folly of the Cross* (Collegeville, MN: The Liturgical Press, 1996) 235-273.

become "one flesh" with Him. We become not only the *adopted* children of God, but the very "*blood* brothers and sisters" to Christ. His Blood now courses through our veins. We are one with Him "by participation" in exactly the same way He is one with Father and Spirit "by nature."

A major problem in overcoming these obstacles to a proper Pauline (and therefore "mystical") understanding of Christ Jesus as Savior is our tendency to treat as metaphorical (and therefore as "unreal" or "less than real") images and symbols that Scripture uses ontologically. Consider, for example, this key text from St. Paul's Letter to the Ephesians (1:3-10):

> *God chose us in Him*
> *Before the world began*
> *To be holy and blameless in His sight*
> *He predestined us to be His adopted sons*
> *Through Jesus Christ,*
> *Such was His will and pleasure,*
> *That all might praise the glorious favor*
> *He has bestowed on us in His beloved.*
>
> *In Him and through His blood*
> *We have been redeemed,*
> *And our sins forgiven*
> *So immeasurably generous*
> *Is God's favor to us.*
>
> *God has given us the wisdom*
> *To understand fully the mystery,*
> *The plan He was pleased to decree in Christ*
> *A plan to be carried out*
> *In Christ, in the fullness of time,*
> *To bring all things into one in him,*
> *In the heavens and on the earth.*

What would it mean to take "God chose us before the world began" as something more than a metaphorical nicety about "God loving us unconditionally"? What would it mean to appreciate our status as "adopted sons and daughters" as something more than "symbolic step-children"? What would it mean to interpret "[I]n Him and through His blood we have been redeemed" as something more real than the tawdry metaphor of forensic exchange it has come to imply? Most importantly, what would it mean to actually believe we have been "given the wisdom to understand fully the mystery, the plan He was please to decree in Christ…a plan to be carried out in Christ in the fullness of time, to bring all things into one in him, in the heavens and on the earth"?

These important questions beg for an answer. What does it mean for something to be "carried out in Christ"? What is meant by "the fullness of time"? How are "all things" to be brought "in to one in Christ"? How can "things" be "brought into" a person, even a Divine Person? These are additional questions that summon the imagination and hearts of those who seek, with St. Paul, to enter into the mysterious depths of the Alpha and the Omega.

# CORPUS TRI-FORME

*A*s we begin to explore a "participatory" understanding of living "in Christ," we must deepen our sense that "incorporation into" Jesus precedes and transcends our efforts to "imitate Christ." Our desire for "intimacy with" Christ must take precedence over our willingness to "follow" Jesus. Our hunger and thirst to be "possessed of and by" Christ must become more important than our feeble attempts simply to "please" Jesus.

As our interior conversion deepens, we begin to notice a very important fact: *Jesus is never alone.* For all eternity, Jesus has never been "just Jesus." Or, to put the mystery more mystically: Jesus exists *only in communion with* the others who, inseparable with Him, constitute His very identity as Son of God. His is a *Communio Personarum* that includes ourselves, as well as the Father and the Holy Spirit. It also includes the entire cosmos (cf. Rom. 8:19-22). Even non-human reality Jesus recapitulates in Himself. It takes a lifetime of contemplative prayer to get our minds and hearts around the mystery of Jesus as a Divine Person who is "ever-in-communion."

Jesus is the *"Corpus Mysticum"* spoken of by St. Paul: the Divine Person whose Mystical Body includes all those "chosen in Him before the foundation of the world" (Eph. 1:4). The Mystery of God's Plan, as we have seen, is to "unite all things in him, things in heaven and things on earth" (Eph. 1:10). This is process continues until, in "the fullness of time...he has put all things under his feet and made him the head over all things for the church, which is his body, the fullness of him who fills all in all" (Eph. 1:10, 22-23).

We can now begin to see how the "fullness of Christ" includes all those predestined by Him to "complete" Himself (Eph. 2:6). Just as

Jesus was never without the Father, and the Father is never not with the Son, so the Son is never without those whom He has chosen complete His mystical Body, the Church (Acts 9:4; Col. 1:15-16, 24; Rom. 12:4-5; 1 Cor. 6:12-20; 10:17; 12:12-27). To be "in Christ," then, is to be incorporated into His *Corpus Mysticum* and to enjoy a real share in His Divine-manhood. This miracle of "participation in Christ" flows from, and is a function of, the Trinitarian form of His love. It is precisely because "God can be one with the other Divine Persons in himself, he is just as capable, in his freedom, of becoming one with the others outside of himself."[46]

Henri de Lubac has shown that "*Corpus Mysticum*" – the Mystery of the Mystical Body of Christ – was a term that in the first twelve centuries of the Church, following the teaching of St. Paul, referred primarily to *the Eucharistic* Mystery. Only subsequently did it come to refer to the "Mystical Body" of the *Church*.[47] The Mystery of Jesus, therefore, was seen by the Fathers as essentially "*Tri-forme*," including (1) the historical Jesus, (2) the Eucharistic Christ, and (3) the Ecclesial Christ, Head and members. The body of Christ born of the Virgin, crucified, died, resurrected, and ascended into heaven, is given to us "mystically" in the *Corpus Mysticum* of the Eucharist for the purpose of creating and sustaining His corporate *Corpus Mysticum*, the Church. Jesus institutes the Eucharist, and the Eucharist creates the Church. The *Corpus Mysticum* of the Church realizes itself through participation in the *Corpus Mysticum* of the Eucharist.

This three-fold (*tri-forme*) mystery of the *Corpus Mysticum* can be glimpsed in Jesus' words, "That they may be one, as You, Father, are in Me, and I in You; that they may be one in Us, that the world may believe that You have sent Me" (Jn. 17:21). Here we see the Trinitarian *perichoresis* being shared with those whom Jesus intends to incorporate into Himself. The Eucharist is the *Corpus Mysticum* of Jesus' Body and

---

[46] Von Balthasar, *Epilogue*, trans. Edward T. Oakes (San Francisco: Ignatius Press, 2004), 86.

[47] Henri de Lubac, *Corpus Mysticum: The Eucharist and the Church in the Middle Ages – A Historical Survey* (London: SCM Press, 2006).

Blood. This Mystery, in turn, generates the *Corpus Mysticum* of His Body, the Church. Today we think of the "Mystical Body of Christ" primarily as the Church. Yet, it is the *Eucharistic* Christ who is the Original *Corpus Mysticum*. By giving Himself to us in the Eucharist, the Eternal Word creates the *fullness* of His *Corpus Mysticum*, which is also called His Bride, the *Ecclesia,* or the Church.

The fontal mystery of the Eucharist and the Church is the *essential relationality* of Jesus Christ. We are tempted to think of Jesus, whether as the Eternal Word or as the "carpenter's son" (Mk. 6:3), as a singular person. Despite Athanasius' refutation of Arius, who held that "there was a time when Jesus was not," it is difficult, given our fallen way of thinking, not to conceive of Jesus as existing as a separate being, independent of His relation to the Father and the Holy Spirit. It is also difficult, on the historical plane, not to conceive of Jesus as a finite being just like any other human person. He is a man "like us in all things," yes, but He is also a *divine Person,* able to incorporate into Himself all things, including creation and fallen humanity. As God, He is able to do this without compromise, change, or dissolution of His divine-human identity. In fact, His identity *does* include fallen humanity and creation (1 Cor. 15:28). He is always in the process of "recapitulating" (renewing, restoring) us as a gift to His Father. As human persons, we are capacitated by Him to "enter into Him" in the same way He exists in relation to His Father and the Holy Spirit. It is His desire, even more so than ours, that we enter into and enjoy this inseparable relationship (Lk. 22:15; John 17:23) with the Persons of the Trinity. The "burning heart" of the Sacred Heart of Jesus is an apt image of His desire that "we may all be made one in Him" (Jn.14:20).

It is important to remember that this "unity" or "union" with Christ is not in any sense artificial. It is not external, forensic, or secondary to the real identity of Jesus. It is neither metaphorical nor analogical. It is essentially mystical. It is real. Here again, "mystical" means "more real than what we comprehend empirically." Jesus has "need" of us in a way that is somehow "essential" to His very identity, both as God and as man.

For reasons we will never fully understand, Jesus has chosen to

59

make us, in a certain sense, *indispensable* to His fullness divine Person. Our union with Him is intimate and organic (cf. John 15:1-11). St. Paul goes so far as to insist, we "make up in our own flesh what is lacking in the sufferings of Christ" (Col. 1:24). We see here our elective, yet ingredient relationship with Jesus as His co-redeemers. It has pleased Him, in some very real yet mysterious sense, "to have need" of us. It's as if the Living Water (John 4:10) has a greater thirst (cf. John 19:28) than those who thirst for Him, to satisfy their thirst (cf. John 7:38). This "need" or "thirst" in Christ *is an essential dimension* of Who Jesus Is, both as God and as man. We somehow "complete" Jesus in a way determined and comprehended only by Him. His *Corpus Mysticum*, the Church, is Jesus Christ Himself, "come to full stature" (Eph. 4:13).

The Little Flower, St. Therese of Lisieux, Doctor of the Church, proclaimed this same amazing truth. Though God can do all things without the help of human beings, she insisted, it has pleased Him to do nothing without us. The patristic tradition goes even further. It asserts that Christ associates us with Himself, both in His mission of redemption and in His relationship with the Father and the Holy Spirit (cf. John 17:11). Our connection to Jesus goes to the very "heart" of Who Jesus is as a divine Person. As members of His *Corpus Mysticum*, we enjoy exactly the same *kind* of constitutive relationship with Jesus as do His Father and the Holy Spirit. Our relationship is not identical to theirs "by nature" but it is identical to theirs "by participation."

As we continue to contemplate the meaning of "participation" "in Christ," we discover, in prayer, what it means to be as "close" to Him as are the other Persons of the Trinity. We begin to perceive that we are somehow "essential" to Who Jesus is in His intimacy with the Father and the Holy Spirit. We begin to be astounded by the fact that He "needs" us – i.e., He has "chosen to need" us – in the same way He has always "needed" and "been one with" the Father and the Holy Spirit. As Balthasar says, "The Church is integral to the form of Christ when that form is understood, as it should be, from this larger Trinitarian perspective...the righteousness (*sedek*) of the Old Testament, as relatedness affecting the whole of man's being...[is] transcended and deepened to a communication to the creature of the relationality of the triune life what affects the whole of being within the Godhead."[48] This "partaking of the divine nature" (2 Pt. 1:4) is made possible by His power as God. He wishes to include us, to enfold us, to incorporate us, in His communion of surrender within the Trinity. "In Christ" we become divine "by participation," in a way that Father, Son, and Spirit are divine "by nature."

Only by repeating and reworking this mystery of *deification* can the enormity of the intimacy with Himself that Christ has predestined for us begin to dawn on our fallen minds and hearts. *Jesus is never alone.* Whether in His identity facing heavenward with the Father and the Holy Spirit, or in His identity facing towards the earth through His relationship with us, the Mystery is the same: Jesus is Who He Is *only in coinherent intimacy and union with* those He has created to be His from all eternity. "He has predestined us to be his adopted sons, such was His will and pleasure, that all might praise the glorious favor He has bestowed on us in His Beloved" (Eph. 1:6).

What is this "glorious favor"? It is nothing short of a real share in the divinity of Christ! During the Eucharistic celebration the priest prays, "Through this mingling of water and wine *may we come to share in the divinity of Christ* who humbled Himself to share in our humanity" (emphasis added). Jesus implies the same thing when He confronts the unbelieving Jews who took offense that He claimed equality with God by saying "Is it not written in your law, 'I said, "You are gods"?'" (Jn. 10:35, quoting Ps. 83:6). In effect, Jesus is saying: "If those who have received this honor ["ye are gods"] by 'participating' in Me, how can I who have this [status of being God] by nature deserve to be

---

[48] Joseph Fessio S.J. and John Riches, ed. *Glory of the Lord: A Theological Aesthetics, volume 1, Seeing the Form,* trans. Erasmo Leiva-Merikakis, (San Francisco: Ignatius Press, 1982) 540 and *Glory of the Lord: A Theological Aesthetics, volume 7, Theology: The New Covenant,* trans. Brian McNeil, ed. John Riches (San Francisco: Ignatius Press, 1989) 311, quoted in W. T. Dickens, *Hans Urs von Balthasar's Theological Aesthetics: A Model for Post-Critical Biblical Interpretation* (Notre Dame, IN: University of Notre Dame Press, 2003) 145.

rejected?"[49] In other words, Jesus affirms *our* deification, even as He affirms His own divinity. Indeed, His divinity is obliquely affirmed by the possibility of our deification. Only God could divinize humans. Jesus, therefore, must be God if He is the Source of our deification. We who are incorporated into Christ and partake of His divine nature (2 Pt. 1:4) can rightly be called "gods," precisely because Jesus, who affirms our divinization in Him, is God. These two mystical truths are indissolubly linked.

---

[49] A favorite argument of St. John Chrysostom to demonstrate both the divinity of Christ and the deification of man.

# CHRISTUS TOTUS

he economy (*Economia*) of the "whole Christ" (*Totus Christus*) includes not only fallen humanity but all of creation as well (Rom. 8:19ff.). Jesus is essentially relational in a way that goes beyond even deifying us in Himself. "The whole creation itself will be set free from its bondage to decay and obtain the glorious liberty of the children of God" (Rom. 8:21). Jesus is the Savior "of the world (Jn. 4:42)." The world He redeems includes the "lamb and the lion," the "scorpion and the adder" (cf. Isa. 11:8). Salvation will be complete when Christ is "all in all" (Col. 3:11).

The corporate nature of Christ Jesus is also eschatological. He is the Alpha and the Omega, the Beginning and the End. All of history, as well as nature, are included in His mission as Redeemer. He is the Savior of the world and the Lord of history. The story of the world finds its interpretive key and fulfillment in Him. The Bible may be seen as the narrative of the progressive fulfillments that occur in Christ. The sequence of salvation history is inherently dramatic. It is a divine *Theodrama*, not simply an organic unfolding, like an acorn becoming an oak. It is a mystery play in which God is Author (Father), Protagonist (Son), and Director (Spirit).[50] Every chapter is a new surprise. God is "ever more." Jesus is utterly unique. Human freedom is never compromised. Human decisions always have consequences. Human choices make a difference to God. In the end, the Lord makes all things redound unto the good of those who love Him (Rom. 8:28). Salvation history is the theological drama involving two freedoms, those of God and man. These freedoms are orchestrated by God to bring to completion the

---

[50] See Von Balthasar's *Theo-Drama: Theological Dramatic Theory, volume 1, Prologomena*, trans. Graham Harrison (San Francisco: Ignatius Press) 268-308.

restoration of the original communion He promised to Adam after the fall (Gen. 3:15).

Jesus Christ enters the Theo-drama of creation and human history as its central Actor in order to reconcile all things to His Father. He comes to recapitulate and restore fallen creation. He comes to redeem humanity and the world from the powers of evil. He comes to present a restored creation to His Father as a gift. Jesus is the Happy Ending for which all of creation and history is yearning.

To better understand this "eschatological economy"[51] and how it is taken up into the *Christus Totus*, we do well to recall the Bible view of creation and history. Unlike secular scientists and historians, biblical authors see the sustaining yet non-interfering hand of God in every chapter of both nature and history. "In the beginning God created the heavens and the earth" (Gen. 1:1). The very first verse of the Scripture reveals to us that God created the cosmos and everything within it as something good. He intended from all eternity that His world be an expression and extension of His love for the creatures He made. All of creation is meant to exist in perfect harmony and communion with itself and with God, its Creator.

Some of the creatures God created, however, – first the angels, then Adam and Eve – doubted God's desire for *communio* with them. They lost their trust in God's goodness. Tempted to self-deification, they misused the freedom God had given them to be in perfect harmony with Him. Their loss of faith resulted in disobedience and death. They broke communion and direct communication with God. Their separation from Him resulted in every form of chaos, disease, and disharmony. Before their fall from grace, they stood before God and before each other "naked without same" (Gen. 2:25). Following their doubt and disobedience, however, they were covered with shame and guilt and needed to clothe themselves in tree leaves and animal skins (Gen. 3:7, 21). The Original Unity they enjoyed with each other and with God was lost. This Fall was so tragic that every last atom of

---

[51] See Douglas H. Knight, *The Eschatological Economy: Time and the Hospitality of God* (Grand Rapids, MI: William B. Eerdmans Publishing Company, 2006).

creation was adversely affected by the sin of Adam and Eve. Entropy (deterioration and decay) entered the world where before there had only been Energy. Death entered the world where there had only been Life. The Life of the world was lost and needed to be restored.

Immediately in the wake of the Fall, God promised a Redeemer. The Lord could not abide, it seems, estrangement from the cosmos and creatures He had made us for intimacy with Himself. In a *proto-evangelium* – an anticipatory gospel – God prophesies to the serpent who tempted Adam and Eve, "I will put enmity between you and the woman, and between your seed and her seed; he shall bruise your head, and you shall bruise his heel" (Gen. 3:15). He predicts a Deliverer who will conquer the evil one and restore creation to its original communion.

To spark this drama of deliverance, God calls a man named Abraham to be the "father of a great nation" (Gen. 12:2). From the seed of Abraham, God's salvation of the world will emerge (Gen. 12:3; 15:4; 17:5). Because of his obedient response of faith to the call of God, Abraham is regarded and declared by God as righteous (Gen. 15:6; cf. Rom. 4:1-15; Heb. 11:8). Abraham is acknowledged as being a "just" man because of his trust in God. He is "justified" – acknowledged as "righteous" before God – because of his obedient faith. He is living in "right relationship" with the Lord who chose him for covenantal commitment. He becomes the model of those who will be found, and declared to be, "righteous" "in Christ."

From the "seed of Abraham," God creates a further *koinonia* with the descendents of Jacob (Gen. 35:10-23). A *communio* of twelve tribes is fashioned by God to be the on-going instrument of His final restoration of the entire human family. In the people of Israel, God strives to recapitulate the whole of fallen creation. Through His chosen people, He seeks to reconcile a rebellious world with himself. The Old Testament may be seen as the account of the Lord's efforts to re-establish the cosmos to its original perfection, using patriarchs, priests, prophets, and kings as His chosen instruments. Creation and Covenant are the inner and outer forms of God's salvific communion with the creatures He has fashioned for Himself

To Moses, one of the specially chosen leaders of His holy people,

God gives the Law (Torah) as both a sign and instrument of Israel's special relationship with Himself. Israel is to gather as a single Person around the Law to be a sign and catalyst for bringing creation and humankind back into *communio* with the God of "Abraham, Isaac, and Jacob." The Law is both a symbol of Israel's election and an instrument of her mission. Her mission is to be "a light unto the nations" (Isa. 42:6; 66:18) and to act as a divine magnet drawing all living creatures back into perfect *koinonia* with their Creator.

Israel, however, failed in her mission. The "works of the law," intended originally as an instrument of recapitulation (restoration), came to be used by the Jews as an excuse for national elitism.[52] Originally meant to be a means of bringing all nations back into communion with God, keeping "the works of the law" became an end in itself. Israel became sectarian rather than universalistic in its self-understanding. Adherence to the "works of the law" came to embody Jewish exclusivism instead of functioning as God's instrument of catholic inclusion. This resulted in a sectarianism and haughty nationalism that was the very opposite of how God intended it to serve. It would therefore "be taken away from you and given to another" (Mt. 21:43).

In the fullness of time, the God of Abraham, Isaac, and Jacob, the God of Moses, Elijah and the prophets, sent His own beloved Son - Jesus - into the world, so that "believing in Him, all might have life in His Name" (Jn. 20:31; cf. 1:12; 5:24). He is the Light (Jn. 8:12) and Life (Jn. 6:51; 9:5) of the world. Jesus replaces the Torah with Himself.[53] He proves capable of doing what Israel did not: "draw all men to Myself" by "being lifted up" (Jn. 12:32). In His Paschal Mystery, Jesus exercises the faithfulness to the Father that God's chosen people were unable to demonstrate. *In His very Person* Jesus is the New Covenant through which all persons can "be saved and come to knowledge of the truth" (1 Tim. 2:4).

---

[52] For this "New Perspective on Paul," see N.T. Wright, *The Climax of the Covenant* (Minneapolis: Fortress Press, 1993).

[53] See Benedict XVI, *Jesus of Nazareth* (San Francisco: Ignatius Press, 2007), esp. chapter 3.

"Participating in Christ," then, means entering *into Jesus' own faithfulness* before God.[54] It is Christ's righteousness before the Father that is our justification. By accepting His invitation to *koinonia*, we enter into *communio*, not only with Jesus, but also with the Father and the Holy Spirit. In this act of faith, we are also one with all those who are "united in Christ" (Col. 2:2). Our communion is both vertical and horizontal. "In Christ," we are taken up into His eternal relationship with the Father and the Holy Spirit. We are also assimilated into a mystical bond with all His "adopted children."

We must not be put off by the term "adopted." Adoption in Christ does not mean, as our fallen understanding may tempt us believe, "secondary" or "not natural." We are not step-children of the Lord; rather, we are members of His own Body, and therefore *heirs* to the Kingdom of His Father (Rom. 8:17). As understood by the early church fathers, divine "adoption" conveys a meaning more profound than its biological or legal equivalents. It communicates an "engrafting" or "incorporation" into a new and better relationship with Christ, one that is deep and permanent, never artificial or arbitrary. To be adopted into the family of God is to be *taken up into* the very Life of the Trinity itself. It is essentially an act of ascension. It is being enfolded into the family of His Elect in a way that makes natural, human blood ties appear anemic by comparison. Our true home is in God, and our true family is the Church. "Participation in Christ" is no mere metaphor. When this realization becomes more important to us than the pious clichés urging us to "do good and avoid evil," we will have grasped the great mystery of the *Totus Christus* for which Christ has "chosen us before the foundation of the world" (Eph. 1:4).

Of a piece with getting beyond a flimsy metaphorical, to a truly mystical, understanding of "participating in Christ" is learning to appreciate the Church as His "Mystical Body." We have already seen

---

[54] For an important and interesting introduction to the New Perspective on St. Paul that includes a re-interpretation of traditionally Protestant positions on imputed righteousness, see Richard B. Hays, *The Faith of Jesus Christ: The Narrative Structure of Galatians 3:1-4:11 (2ⁿᵈ edition)* (Grand Rapids, MI: William B. Eerdmans Publishing Company, 2002).

how, for the early Church, the Eucharist was the *Corpus Mysticum* of Christ, creating and unifying His larger *Corpus Mysticum*, the Church. The Church is the "place of rebirth" where persons become "new creations" (2 Cor. 5:17) in Christ.[55] The Church itself must be seen as the primordial *Sacrament* of Salvation.

What is a sacrament? It is an efficacious *sign* that contains, embodies, conveys, communicates, and manifests the invisible mystery to which it points. The Church is a living Sign that *contains within it* the fullness of the Mystery of Christ. It reveals and conceals the Lord to whom it points. Every sacramental sign finds its fullness in the reality which it proclaims, even while "participating" in that same reality of which it serves as a sign. As the primordial Sacrament of Christ among us, the Church finds its fullness in the Kingdom of God, but it also manifests the Kingdom of God on earth. The Church *is* the Kingdom of God on earth, even while awaiting its consummation and completion in the Wedding Feast of the Lamb (Rev. 19:9). To put the matter differently: heaven is already on earth in the Church, and the earthly Church awaits its final perfection in the fullness of heaven.

We see, then, that the Church is not brought into being for Herself alone. She is given "for the life of the world." Just as Israel was called forth from the seed of Abraham to be "light unto the nations," so the *Corpus Mysticum* of the Church is called into being through the Paschal Mystery of Jesus "to fulfill and complete" what Israel did not accomplish. The Church is the Spouse of the Savior – the Second Eve wedded to the Second Adam – achieving in the New Dispensation what Israel failed to achieve in the First.

The *Totus Christus* is brought to His fullness in the Wedding Feast of the Lamb (Rev. 19:9). The *Corpus Mysticum* of the Church, like the *Corpus Mysticum* of the Eucharist that creates it, is a means to an end. The Eucharistic *Ekklesia* is the Incarnation of Christ mystically expanded through time. Jesus of Nazareth, in His Paschal Mystery,

---

[55] For an inspiring treatment of the Church as the "Place of Rebirth," see Olivier Clement, *The Roots of Christian Mysticism: Texts from the Patristic Era with Commentary* (Hyde Park, NY: New City Press, 1993) 95-124.

bequeaths to us His *Corpus Mysticum* as Eucharist. The celebration of the Eucharist generates His *Corpus Mysticum* the Church. His *Corpus Mysticum,* the Church, functions as a divine source of unity, gathering all nations unto itself. The culmination of the Eucharistic Church is the Wedding Feast of the Lamb. The Kingdom of God in heaven is the eschatological fullness of the Eucharistic Sacrifice. The Eucharistic *Ekklesia* both anticipates and manifests the Wedding Feast of the Lamb in the Kingdom of God.

This vision of Jesus as *Corpus Tri-forme* and of His Body as *Corpus Mysticum* shows Jesus as coming from the Father to gather all things to Himself and to re-present them to the Father. He gathers up and "recapitulates" a fallen cosmos and humanity and delivers it back to His Father, restored to a condition even more beautiful than that prior to the Fall. The Holy Spirit orchestrates and brings about this "economy of salvation." He repairs and restores broken Creation in the Incarnation. He reunites the broken human race by gathering it together and uniting it in the Eucharistic *Ekklesia.* Scripture is fulfilled in the Church, and the Church is fulfilled in the Wedding Feast of the Lamb.

The Church, therefore, is essentially a sacrament of the Ascension. To live in Christ's *Corpus Mysticum* is to participate in both the Resurrection and Ascension of Christ. It is to be indissolubly united with Him in His very Person. It is already to be seated with Him at the "right hand of the Father" (Col. 3:1), for "God who is rich in mercy... raised us up with Him and made us sit with Him in the heavenly places" (Eph. 2:6). "Your life is hidden with God in Christ (Col. 3:3), St. Paul tells us. This means we abide with Him now, in the fullness of His glory, even though we still "walk by faith not by sight" (2 Cor. 5:7). United to the *Totus Christus* in His *Corpus Mysticum,* our real lives are in heaven, even though we still live and labor here on earth.

# PART TWO

## Human Personhood

*Section One*

# *Alterity*

# THEONOMY: THE ACTING PERSON

*O*nly a person can truly "act." Persons who have not fully realized themselves as persons can only "re-act." There is a world of difference between truly, and freely, acting as a person, and simply "re-acting" to the events and circumstances that impinge upon us.

Taking a cue from the tile of Karol Wojtyla's (Pope John Paul II's) philosophical work, *The Acting Person*, we will now explore the mystery of the human person considered as a person capable of "acting," not just "re-acting." "[O]nly the person in sole possession of himself can be a person," says Wojtyla.[56] This comment raises some important questions: What can be said about the person who is "fully in possession of" himself or herself? What does it mean to "be in possession of" one's self? How can the self "own" the self? Doesn't love mean sacrificing the self for the sake of the other? Aren't we meant to live in communion with each other, giving our selves away in order to make others happy? Isn't self-possession just another term for selfishness? These are the sorts of questions we encounter when we consider the mystery of the acting person.

Our approach here mirrors our contemplation of the Persons of the Trinity. Human persons reflect (image forth) and participate in the ontologically personal nature of the Trinitarian *Hypostases*. Created in the image and likeness of this Three-Person Mystery, we share in the unity-in-difference that constitutes the nature of the Triune God. True human personhood, then, is "theonomous." It is a manifestation in miniature of the "inseparable yet unmixed" mystery of the Trinitarian Persons.

---

[56] Karol Wojtyla, *The Acting Person* (Dortrecht, Holland: D. Reidel Publishing Company, 1979) 105.

Focusing on the human person as one who fulfills himself or herself in action, Karol Wojtyla tells us, is the best entrée into understanding the mystery of the human person. Action, he insists, requires self-possession. One cannot "give one's self away" authentically (freely, maturely) without first somehow "being in possession of one's self." Engaging in self-surrender before achieving self-control is not truly making a "gift of one's self." It is more akin to a "selling short" of one's self, perhaps even a prostitution of one's self. Making a genuine self-gift of one's self – the only way to self-fulfillment, in Wojtyla's view – requires a prior "possession" of one's self. So important is this acquisition of self-possession that, according to Wojtyla, a person lacking it cannot be called a person in the fullest sense of the word.

Immediately the question arises: are we persons in our own right before being able to "act freely," or is personhood something we *acquire* as we learn to act as self-possessed human beings? What is the difference between simply "being human" and "becoming a person"? In what sense does anyone ever "become" a human person? Isn't personhood something *given* us at the moment of conception? Aren't fetuses in the womb fully human persons? In what sense is personhood dependent upon learning how to become "an acting person?"

Each of these questions could involve us in endless philosophical speculation that would prove uninspiring and unconvincing, though many a great Catholic philosopher has pondered and written about these questions extensively. I will be focusing on selected aspects of these questions that derive from the light and beauty of the Trinitarian *Hypostases* as discussed in chapter one. Since the human person is created in the *imago Dei*, everything we can say truthfully about the human person comes from Christological truth rooted in the Trinity. *Jesus reveals us to ourselves.* It is not philosophical insight that we are after, but Christological light shining on the mystery of the human person.

In the section entitled, "The Triumph of Hypostasis," we discussed the absolute "otherness" (alterity) of each of the Trinitarian Persons. God's "Being" (*ousia*), we said, is utterly and ontologically "personal." There is no "Being" in God that is not defined by the personal otherness of each of the Persons in the divine *Communio Personarum*. Now we can explore the same ontological mystery in the human *communio personarum*.

The irreducibility of the Persons in the immanent Trinity is imaged forth in the human family. No two human persons are the same. Each is ineluctably different and altogether unsubstitutable. This is a direct reflection of the manner in which the Persons within the Trinity Who are "unmixed and unconfused." Each and every human person is as utterly unique, incommunicable, and non-transferable as each of the Divine *Hypostases*. Just as the Father is never the Son, the Son never the Father, and the Spirit never either of the others, no single human person is ever comparable to or interchangeable with another human person. True, similarities exist: we can discern a kind of "nature" or "species" that may be said to characterize the "whole human race." But, when it comes down to particular, specific persons, no two human persons are any more alike than are the Trinitarian Persons within their own differentiated unity. Our thesis here is fairly radical: *the human person, considered in and of himself or herself, is just as much a mystery, as each of the Persons of the Trinity*, calling for a similar (though not equal) reverence, respect, and devotion we give to Father, Son, and Holy Spirit. "Whatever you do to the least of these, my brethren, you do unto me" (Mt. 25:40). The dignity of the human person, created in the image and likeness of the Trinity, derives from his or her "participation" in the *Communio Personarum* who created them.

The selfhood of the human person is also a "transcendent autonomy."[57] The human person considered in and of herself is totally free, wholly autonomous, and completely "other." At the same time, every unique, autonomous person (*hypostasis*) fulfills, actualizes, completes, and realizes himself *in communion with* other persons (*hypostases*) who are also completely "other" and totally unique. This is the mystery of the transcendent selfhood of the human person. It reflects, derives from, and reveals the Trinitarian Mystery of the Three Person God.

---

[57] In this section I follow the brilliant phenomenology of John Crosby, *The Selfhood of the Human Person* (Washington, D.C.: The Catholic University of America Press, 1966), chapter 3.

Focusing in this section on the *autonomous* character of the human person, we see, in the light of the unique *Hypostases* within the Trinity, that each human person is "without confusion" and "unmixed." No person can be fully identified with any other person, project, activity, or role to which we might be tempted to reduce them. Confusing someone with someone or something other than themselves is to "de-personalize" them. Viewing someone as something other than the singular mystery that they are is to obscure the beauty of their unrepeatable personhood. Slavery, for example, radically de-personalizes persons. So too does prostitution. Killing people we deem unfit to live, whether in the womb, in the laboratory, or at the end of life, is the most extreme form of de-personalization. In all of these examples we see that treating persons as mere "specimens" of any "category" strips them of their dignity. Our appreciation of them as "persons" is driven out the moment we see them as "members" in what is thought to be a prior and more important "species." The mystery of the human person cannot be reduced either to species membership or to any other quality or excellence we might believe "defines" a person.

This also includes trying to define human person in relation to human nature itself. Just as the Persons (*Hypostases*) within the Trinity are not reducible to "the divine nature" (*ousia*), human persons are not adequately described simply as individual "human beings." The classical definition of the human person as "an individual substance of a rational nature" (*persona est substantia individual naturae rationalis*) does not do justice to *the singular mystery* of the human person. A person is never merely an individual. A person is always an ineluctable mystery, wholly unique unto one's self.

Professor John Crosby identifies four things we must bear in mind in seeking to understand the mystery of human personhood. First, *persons are always ends-in-themselves.* They are never instruments or mere means to what are believed to be greater ends. Second, *persons are always "wholes" of their own.* They are never simply "parts" of some larger totality or collectivity. Third, *persons are inherently "incommunicable."* They are never only specimens of some wider "genus" or category. Fourth, *each person "belongs" to himself or herself alone.* They are never "possessed" or "owned" by the other(s).[58] Thus, persons *"stand in themselves,* and exist for their own sakes. In an incomparable sense are themselves and not any other. They belong first and foremost to themselves.

It is only because of this irreducible and incommunicable selfhood that persons are most fully alive when they function as "acting persons." For only persons whose identities are not mingled with or collapsed into those of others can act through themselves."[59] A person's acts are radically their own because the essence of their personhood cannot be attributed to another. This has enormous implications for human behavior and moral culpability. Blaming, scapegoating, excuse-making, and every other form of personal disownership disappear when it comes to accounting for the responsibility of the acting person. As John Paul II reminds us, following the Scholastic axiom *agree sequitur esse* (acting follows being), "as a person is, so do they act." "I," and no one else, account for my actions. This is because "I," and no one else, is "me."

The "mystery of me" may sound "egotistical" or "selfish." This is a profoundly mistaken, but most common, notion. It is inherently un-Christian and anti-Trinitarian. In a later section we will discuss at greater length the ambiguities of the concept of *self-sacrifice* in a Christian context. For the moment we will simply note some examples of the saints whose "ownership" of their actions help reveal the mystery of the human person, as well as the *humility,* involved in appropriating the "mystery of me."

Jacques Maritain has observed[60] that the saints virtually never acted on maxims or commandments that applied equally to all persons, regardless of temperament or disposition. They invariably acted in ways singularly unique to themselves. No two saints were ever alike in the manner in which they responded to the call of the gospel. In so doing, the saints reveal to us that persons, *qua persons*, impress their *personal incommunicability* upon their moral acts and goodness. Conversely, their

---

[58] Crosby, *Selfhood of the Human Person* (Washington, DC: Catholic University of America Press, 1996) 14-21.

[59] Crosby, *Selfhood of the Human Person*, 35.

[60] Quoted in Crosby, *Selfhood of the Human Person*, 241.

moral examples of courage and faith express and disclose their personal uniqueness.

Thus, St. Thomas More (as portrayed in Robert Bolt's play, *A Man For All Seasons*) says to his friend, Norfolk, when asked to account for his stubbornness in not taking the Oath giving King Henry VIII rights over the Church in England: "I will not give in because *I* oppose it – *I do* – not my pride, not my spleen, nor any other of my appetites *but I do – I!*"[61] Similarly, John Henry Cardinal Newman spoke of how "egotism," understood properly, "is true modesty."[62] No one can speak for me. I am the author of my own words, my own actions. No person other than me can assume responsibility for my behavior. The person I am expresses itself in my actions. In turn, the actions I engage in shape, determine, and reveal my character as a person. We grievously misconceive humility, sanctity, and personhood whenever we think of these apart from the way in which each person is incommunicably himself or herself.

To appreciate the "acting person," then, we must view persons as always acting "through themselves." They are never merely "undergoing" things or "enduring" even difficult circumstances. They "belong to themselves," no matter where they are or what they are doing, undergoing, or suffering. Persons are forever a mystery to themselves, as well as to others. Theirs is a "mysterious concreteness." Persons are never mere "instances" or "examples" of a more fundamental pool, group, or class of qualities. They are "anchored in themselves." They are always "*sui iuris*" ("one of a kind"). They "belong" to themselves. They "stand" in themselves. They are "gathered" in themselves. They are, as Newman put it, "as whole and independent a being in [themselves], as if there were no [others] in the world but [them]."[63] The human person is, in his or her own way, as great a mystery as the Trinitarian Persons in whose inconceivable image and likeness he or she is created.

---

[61] Robert Bolt, *A Man for All Seasons* (New York: Vintage Books, 1990) 38-39 (emphasis added).

[62] John Henry Newman, *A Grammar of Assent* (London: Longmans, Green, and Co., 1898) 384-385.

[63] Cited by Crosby, *Selfhood of the Human Person*, 51.

# HETERONOMY:
## THE REPRESSED PERSON

*A*s we have seen, there are a number of ways in which persons can be de-personalized. In this section we will focus on one such way, the phenomenon of *heteronomy*. Heteronomy refers to the tyranny of the "should." It involves a slavish surrender of the person to external authority. This heteronomous surrender often idealizes itself as admirable "obedience" or a valiant "sense of duty." Heteronomy is always destructive of the human person. Yet, it can disguise itself in the most sanctimonious forms, including certain versions of what Pope Benedict XVI has termed "pious pelagiansim."[64]

Let us begin by looking at two of the most common, non-Christian forms of heteronomic depersonalization. Buddhism, and other New Age, Gnostic religious movements resembling it, promote what might be called the "fulfillment of the self" through the "disappearance of the self." They represent a distinctly inverted ideal of personal "fulfillment." They involve not merely an "overcoming" of the self – whatever that might mean – but an actual "destruction" of the self. The *fulfillment* of the self they strive for lies in the actual *elimination* of the self. The *self* is thought to be an obstacle to personal happiness and fulfillment. The self is believed to be overcome through the annihilation of the unique characteristics of the person, especially his or her intentionality. Personal initiative is identified with ego, and ego is imagined always

---

[64] Joseph Ratzinger, *The Yes of Jesus Christ* (New York, NY: Crossroads Publishing Company, 1991) 81, cited in Tracey Rowland, *Ratzinger's Faith: The Theology of Pope Benedict XVI* (Oxford: University Press, 2008) 77.

and everywhere to be bad. The self is, on this view, fulfilled by learning how to disappear.

In Hinduism and similar monistic religions and philosophies, the self is also said to be fulfilled by disappearing, though by different means. Monistic faiths, unlike the more ethereal Buddhist-like cults, envision fulfillment to occur through the *merging* or *absorption* of the self within a larger totality, like a drop of water dissolving in the immensity of the ocean. Here the self is thought to find fulfillment by *blending in* and disappearing. The world soul absorbs into itself all the individual souls, and the individual soul finds Nirvana by being dissolved without remainder into the soul of the world.

In both Buddhism and Hinduism, and other such pantheistic philosophies, movements, fads, and religious trends, individual and incommunicative personhood is thought to be something inherently evil, needing to be overcome. The ideal here is the elimination of the self. Fulfillment is defined as perfect de-personalization. The particularity of the human person is viewed as intrinsically problematic. Personal specificity represents the main obstacle to personal fulfillment. Personal uniqueness is seen as an impediment to personal holiness. Holiness, on this view, requires the *sacrifice* of personal identity for the sake of a more primordial reality. Perfection means the *destruction* of the person for the triumph of the ideal. Nothingness is heaven. The person is a pen-ultimate reality, destined to be "overcome." Personal particularity is eliminated, either by being merged or evaporated in the service of a larger ideal.

Christianity is sometimes tempted to these same, non-Christian illusions, especially given the language of self-surrender and self-sacrifice that characterizes the gospel (e.g., Mt. 10:39). Christianity is not stoicism, but it is perennially inclined in that direction, as the respective histories of Manichaeism, Albigensenism, Jansenism, and Calvinism readily attest. A certain kind of neo-orthodox Catholicism is also riddled with these impersonal, stoical tendencies. We need a New Evangelization, but not one based on heteronomous or monistic ideals. We need a New Evangelization that rests squarely upon the Christological *kerygma* rooted in the Trinitarian Mystery of Unity-in-difference.

From an authentically Trinitarian perspective, the "self-giving" of the person is always a fulfillment, never a compromise or constriction, of the uniqueness of the human person. The acting person who is "giving" himself or herself in service to others enters into *communio* with them, but always in an "unmixed and unconfused" way. John Paul II describes this dynamic well when he explains why the terms *communio* and *communio personarum* more aptly describe the mystery of relationship than other ways of depicting self-giving and self-donation: "'*Communio*' says more and with greater precision [than 'community'] because *it indicates precisely the 'help' that derives in some way from the very fact of existing as a person 'beside' a person.*"[65] The key word here is "beside." Love is walking with and beside another person, not usurping, eviscerating, or overwhelming the "otherness" of the other. The integrity of the human person, even in the act of self-surrender, reflects and derives from the mystery of the Trinity. Distance and intimacy exist in *direct*, not inverse proportion, within the Trinity. "Leaving the other free is something that goes back to the distance which is established in the begetting [of the Son by the Father]."[66] Self-surrender, therefore, is always an *enhancement*, not an encroachment, of personal alterity within the Trinity. Father, Son, and Holy Spirit eternally give themselves away to each other *without loss* of personal identity. So must human persons who wish to be in communion with each other in ways that are fruitful, free, and fulfilling.

We now begin to see how, from a Trinitarian perspective, Jesus invites us to imitate His singular yet inseparable relationship with the Father and the Holy Spirit. As happens first and foremost in the inner life of the Trinity, the surrender of human persons to each other also results in the mutual enhancement of the unique *hypostases* involved. It never involves a cramping or blending of their separate

---

[65] John Paul II, *Man and Woman He Created Them: A Theology of the Body* trans. Michael Waldstein (Boston: Pauline Media, 2006) 162.
[66] Von Speyr, *The World of Prayer,* 66.

identities. Similarly, true self-giving of human persons never leads to an evisceration, elimination, absorption, or evaporation of who they are in order to create or conform to a more primordial state of union. A self, whether human or divine, must be "in possession" of itself in order to surrender "personally" to the other. Anything less than self-possessed self-surrender is masochism, stoicism, Buddhism, Hinduism, or some other form of pantheistic totalism. These religious forms of heteronomy, often masquerading as ideals of Christian self-giving, represent the death of Trinitarian personalism.

In Christian personalism, each and every person is called into being specially by God and given a name (cf. Isa. 45:3; Rev. 2:17). This name indicates the incommunicability of the human person. I am never not me. In the depths of my being I am *who* I am. The "who" "I am" never changes. I am incommunicable and unrepeatable. I am utterly unique. I am made for communion with others, but I never lose or forfeit my own unsubstitutable *hypostatic* uniqueness. Here we see a connection to that pivotal biblical event when God told Moses His Name: "I am Who am," said YHWH (Ex. 3:14). God's Name is His identity. Just as God is always an indefinable Who, never a What, so are we, at the core of our existence, always and forever irreducibly *persons*.

This is not to imply that the self is God. It is meant to imply that, since we are created as persons in the image and likeness of God, we enjoy our personhood with the same unique unrepeatable *hypostatic* substantiality that God enjoys in each of His divine *Hypostases*. Indeed, this is what it means to be created in His image and likeness. In the "me-ness" of "me," I partake of something of the ineffability of each of the divine Persons, Father, Son, and Holy Spirit.

Something of this unrepeatablity and unavoidability of my "being me and only me" reveals itself in the misguided attempts of idealists to do away with themselves in the name of a higher ideal. If suicide is inverted pride, as Thomas Merton suggests,[67] it is never actually self-destruction. The self can never really destroy itself. It does not enjoy the transcendence of God, enabling it to stand outside itself to decide

---

[67] Thomas Merton, *New Seeds of Contemplation* (New York: New Directions, 1972) 181.

what should become of itself. Suicide is an action that seeks in vain to employ the self to remove the self, but it never really works. On the other side of death, one is faced with the reality of having tried to do away with something – someone – whom God has created. What God created, however, never disappears. Hatred of self only affirms the self, most paradoxically and tragically when the self tries to destroy itself.

Often the despairing self justifies this action by accusing itself of not living up to the ideals appropriated by the self. Instead of simply accepting itself as a created yet fallen creature of the living, loving God, some persons try to annihilate themselves through what ends up being an implicit affirmation of their irreducibility as persons. As a cultural cliché puts it: "wherever I go, there I am." Idealistic attempts to "transcend" the self by escaping the self are absurd on their face and harmful – sometimes deadly - to the persons who pursue such ill-fated ideals.

Jesus' discourse on Himself as the Good Shepherd illustrates the importance of self-possessed relationships. "I am the Good Shepherd," He says. "I lay down my life for my sheep. No one takes my life from me. I lay it down of my own accord. I have the power to lay down my life. I also have the power to take it up again" (John 10:18). Here we see a human being in perfect possession of himself. He is not reacting to external pressure or being driven by other ancillary impulses. He is cooperating freely with the inspirations of the Holy Spirit. He is continually discerning the Will of His Father. As man, Jesus is exhibiting, *in His relationship with Himself*, the giving-and-receiving relationship He has with His Father and the Holy Spirit within the Trinity. His love of the Father and the Holy Spirit is *perichoretic* as well as self-possessed. He is in complete control of Himself, even as he surrenders Himself to the other Persons of the Trinity, as well as to those He encounters in His ministry of salvation.

So too with myself: "I" have a relationship with "myself." I am never merely a human being. I am forever a human person. I am always capable of "taking my life in my own hands." Whether I seek to do away with myself or give my self in love to others, it is always "I" who am doing either the killing or the loving. There is no escaping the inevitability of "me." I am in possession of an interior freedom that is more or less understood, grasped, owned, and developed by my self. How I use my freedom expresses and defines the unique and incommunicable "me" that God has made me to be.

It is very disconcerting to encounter forms of Christian idealism that de-personalize the human self. Despite Jesus' declaration that "I have come that they may have life and have it to the full," (John 10:10) some Christian idealists portrays the Christian life as a diminution of the human person. Well-meaning moralists marshal such biblical verses as "He must become greater, I must become lesser" (John 3:30) to prove the importance of eliminating personal identity in the noble calling of imitating Christ. They cite the Commandments of both Old and New Testaments to stress the importance of unquestioning obedience to a demanding moral code. They solicit the authority of the Church in an attempt to compel submission of personal subjectivity to the objective truth of Sacred Tradition. What are we to make of these ostensibly pious claims enjoining the sacrifice of self on the altar of idealist obedience? How are we to interpret these calls for the submission of the self to a higher authority, commanding and requiring our unconditional consent?

Three of the most difficult terms in the Christian lexicon to interpret aright from a Trinitarian, personalist perspective are: "conscience," "obedience," and "the Will of God." When interpreted in a heteronomous way, these seem to demand the judging and shaming of the human self. They seem to compel the submission of the self to the higher authority of the law-giving God. They seem to require that we jettison what *we* would like to do in favor of what we believe *God* wants us to do. They implicitly picture God as our Adversary, not our Ally. They assume that our desires and God's Will are in eternal opposition. They suggest that "following our conscience" means "giving up our own will." "Doing God's will" is presumed to be the opposite of following our heart's desire. God's Will and our will are imagined to be antithetical, brought into harmony only by "sacrificing our self" and "obeying the dictates of our "conscience."

From a personalist, Trinitarian perspective, however, there is another, more integrated way of interpreting conscience, obedience, and doing God's Will. This way invites us to see that "conscience" is never reducible to "superego."[68] Conscience is better grasped in its true, non-heteronomous meaning as "our heart's deepest desire."[69] Sadly, many well-intention Catholic moralists have not always contemplated the difference between superego and conscience as the Church understands it.[70] The superego commands that acts be performed for someone else's approval. These commands are to be completed or undergone in order to make one acceptable and loveable to the one(s) doing the commanding. Such heteronomous orders generate an underlying fear that if these expectations are not – whether for God, one's parents, the community, the state, etc. – the acceptance offered by these parties will be withdrawn.

Persons dominated by the superego live entirely out of these expectations of others. This inordinate "desire to please" usually results in a paralyzing fear, anxiety, and insecurity. Such persons yields the place in themselves that should be occupied by their own self. They *disown themselves.* They allow themselves, as it were, to be "inhabited" by others whose inarticulate expectations dominate their thinking and deciding faculties. Their own view of the world, if it exists at all, is suppressed in deference to the presumed views of authoritarian others. Though capable of thinking for themselves, such persons remains sheltered in a symbiotic relation with the introjected authority of others. At the deepest level of their being, such persons have not given themselves permissions to think or act for themselves. Their creative energies and spontaneity are crippled by their dependence upon and slavish submission to the introjected other. What looks like docile obedience, perhaps even humility, is actually a disownership of self and a forfeiture

---

[68] See John Crosby, *Personalist Papers*, (Washington, D.C.: Catholic University of America Press, 2004) 93-113. See also John W. Glaser, S.J., "Conscience and Superego: A Key Distinction," Theological Studies, Volume: 32 issue: 1 (February, 1971), 30-47.

[69] See John Dunne, *The Road of the Heart's Desire* (Notre Dame, IN: University of Notre Dame Press, 2002).

[70] See *The Catechism of the Catholic Church* #1778

of one's unique, creative capabilities. These capabilities and personal identity then take a subterranean path, sabotaging the person's attitudes and behaviors, eventually resulting in guilt, shame, remorse, and self-defeating behaviors that further estrange the person from himself.

With true development of "conscience," things are quite different. Responding to our conscience - what Newman called a "magisterial dictate...the aboriginal voice of Christ" within us,[71] - we definitely feel that we will not be able to live with ourselves if we act against our conscience. Conscience exercises what at first glance appears to be a heteronomous influence "over" us. But with conscience I am not *reacting* to the pressure of introjected authoritative persons making extrinsic demands upon me *that I do not understand*. Rather, I am *responding* with interior freedom to moral imperatives *I understand and experience* as *fulfilling of* the person God created me to be. The key difference here is that I have a clearly understood sense of how it is in my own best interests — i.e., how it redounds to my fulfillment as a person — to follow the moral imperatives that *present themselves* to my conscience. I see that God is not "out to get me." I understand clearly that Father, Son, and Holy Spirit desire nothing other than my *perichoretic* union with them. Conscience invites me, even propels me, to act in accordance with *objective values* that I recognize, appreciate, and appropriate as intrinsically connected to my growth and perfection as a person. If there is any guilt in my experience of conscience, it is because I recognize that acting contrary to the "dictates" of my conscience leaves me worse off for my betrayal of the objective values (truths, goods) that are fulfilling of the singular *hypostasis* God has called me to be. The guilt I may feel is proportionate to the importance of the *value* in question. It is also integrated into my future desire to do everything I can to cooperate with God's deepest desires for my life. Instead of the "blind" and fear-driven obedience occasioned by the superego, the obedient response elicited by conscience always has the character

---

[71] John Henry Newman, *An Essay in Aid of a Grammar of Assent* (London: Longmans, Green, and Co., 1898) chapter 5, sect. 1, 105-6, cited in Crosby, *Selfhood of the Human Person*, 102. Cited also in CCC #1778.

of *joyfully and eagerly* responding to a *call*. God always invites, He never forces or imposes. Or, as Balthasar says, "We are not asked; we are invited."[72]

We can contrast the demands of conscience with the panic and tension associated with the artificial pressure applied by the heteronomous demands of the superego. Persons driven by superego often work extra hard at meeting the commands of an external authority. In so doing, however, they turn the good news of Christ into a Manichean facsimile that fails to inspire. They find themselves becoming depressed without knowing how or why. The joy of knowing Jesus is foreign to them. The dourness of the repressed person has overshadowed and darkened the ecstatic openness and eucharistic gratitude of those who live in the light of the risen Christ.

---

[72] Von Balthasar, *The Grain of Wheat: Aphorisms*, 80.

# Autonomy: The Isolated Person (Atomos)

*I*f persons can be de-personalized and their theonomous personhood repressed through heteronomy, they can also be depersonalized through a *radical autonomy* that estranges them from "the innermost center of [their] own existence (*Eigenleben*)."[73] If heteronomy represses human person by prematurely dissolving the uniqueness of the person into a grander scheme of an external ideal, radical autonomy perverts the human person by overestimating the singularity and separateness of the person. It results in isolating, alienating, and estranging the person from himself and others.

*Rugged individualism* is the clearest example of radical autonomy serving as a surrogate for true uniqueness within the human person. To be an "individual," rugged or otherwise, is not to be a fully human person. Within a Trinitarian perspective, there is a world of difference between seeking to affirm myself as "a unique individual," and "standing forth" as an incommunicable human person of unique beauty and goodness. The pursuit of self-esteem has nothing in common with the hypostatic singularity of the human person within the Christian vision.

The desire for radical autonomy can perhaps be seen as a natural over-reaction to the repressive totalism of heteronomous smothering. In a desperate effort to free oneself from the mushy altruism or dictatorial authoritarianism, some persons believe the selfhood of the human person must be affirmed by breaking away from others completely

---

[73] This is a concept developed by Dietrich Von Hildebrand, cited in Crosby, *Selfhood of the Human Person*, 106, to stress the interior freedom and value-driven self-possession characteristic of the mature human person.

and trying to fulfill themselves in radical independence and complete, unfettered autonomy. Ideals of "radical individualism" and the "self-made person" are called upon to legitimate such beliefs. Freedom is then defined as license. Fulfillment is construed as "becoming my own person." Freedom becomes "doing whatever I need to in order to get whatever I want." Suddenly, the person is *isolated* from all relationships. The true ideal of self-possession is twisted into a pursuit of self-interest. When this happens, the mystery of self-discovery morphs demonically into a nightmare of self-aggrandizement. The world becomes my playground, and other persons, my play things. Relationships are seen as impediments to my own self-actualization, and commitments a barrier to self-fulfillment. I believe I am the Captain of my own ship, and – as immature children sometimes cry – "nobody is the boss of me."

This is a tragic state of affairs. In this situation, the individual is no longer a person in the fullest sense of the term. Personhood has been reduced to individuality. But radical individuality is non-being. Personhood alone is life because Jesus alone is "the Way, the Truth, and the Life," and we are created as persons in His image and likeness. Personhood always means *being-in-communion* with others without confusion or loss of personal identity. Becoming a person is always more than being an individual with ego-centric preferences or needing to be the center of attention.

"*Atomos*" is a term that can help us distinguish the isolated individual from the fully alive and intimately related "*hypostasis*," or person.[74] *Atomos* indicates isolation vs. communion, radical individualism vs. personal relationship. When a person is 'atomized," his or her deepest desires are severed from their proper fulfillment in committed relationships. Love degenerates into lust. One's God-given élan for union and intimacy becomes an animal-like possessiveness. It devolves into a desire to consume or control. *Eros* is turned into eroticism, and desire is re-configured into wanton craving. What is meant to be mystical and

---

[74] Olivier Clement develops this term beautifully in his book, *On Being Human: A Spiritual Anthropology* (New York: New City Press, 2000) 10-14.

divine in persons is flattened into mere utilitarianism. The person is reduced to an atomized individual. He or she lives in his or her own little world. Other persons and things become extensions of the isolated self, to be used whenever and however one chooses. Manipulation reigns supreme. What John Paul II called "the personalistic norm"[75] is forgotten altogether. "Freedom of choice" becomes a false replacement for self-possessed decision-making. The only criteria for "free choice" that the *atomos* recognizes is his or her momentary whim or dominating passion. Authentic subjectivity degenerates into crude subjectivism. The pursuit of truth becomes relativistic and therefore "totally irrelevant." Relativism and utilitarianism follow automatically from an atomistic anthropology.

The conversion or "turn around" from living as an *atomos* (individual) to living as a *hypostasis* (person) is as important as it is titanic. It involves a complete and never-ending *metanoia* (turning around) of one's entire being. The surrender needed for such a conversion is not easy to come by. Atomized individuals also have an atomized view of sin. They fail to see that their attitudes and disposition are greater problems for them than the specific misdeeds they may commit. The unacknowledged insolence of the atomistic individuals is a greater affront to the Triune Mystery than their isolated acts of misbehavior. This is why *"metanoia,"* or conversion, is always something larger than merely repenting of individual immoral acts.

Hardened sinners are often closer to real *metanoia* than ostensibly moral individuals. Real sinners like Mary Magdalene and St. Augustine know from bitter experience that they have a desperate need to put their lives on a completely new and different basis. They have tasted the bitter dregs of loveless passion and enervating promiscuity. They know the difference between "craving" and "holy desire." They have experienced in a radical way the disintegration that occurs when *eros* ends in desolation. They have almost died from the disharmony which results when the capacity for self-restraint is surrendered to the pursuit

---

[75] Karol Wojtyla, *Love and Responsibility* (New York, NY: Farrar, Straus and Giroux, Inc., 1981) 40-44.

of self-gratification. They have seen first hand what hell is created when the isolated individual seeks self-fulfillment by exalting the self at the expense of the other. They recognize their own impoverished condition and are ready to seek another solution.

The alternative offered by Christ is anything but a minor adjustment to the atomized person's individual tastes. It involves the total destruction of their individualism (*atomos*) and calls for the re-creation of their personhood (*hypostasis*) in light of the Trinitarian Mystery. Only by looking to the singularity and inseparability *exhibited by Christ in the Life of the Trinity* can we know how atomistic individualism is to be overcome. Conversion always means returning to the Trinity for both the light and the power we need to become the persons God created us to be.

We are now in a position to amplify the meaning of "*transcendent selfhood*." Transcendent selfhood always has two dimensions, subjective and objective. The subjective component is what we have been calling mature self-possession. We must be internally free, recollected, fully "masters" of ourselves in order to be able to make a free gift of ourselves. We must "stand in ourselves" to "be ourselves." To love my neighbor as myself presumes *I have a self* with which to love my neighbor. The Second Great Commandment ("Love your neighbor as yourself") does not call for the elimination of the self or the annihilation of myself. Indeed, love of self is the prerequisite for, even the criteria or measure of, authentic love of another.

At the same time, this love of self will become *atomos* if it is not oriented towards and linked to objects and persons outside (transcending) myself. To be most fully myself, I must also be deliberately and intentionally related to others. This brings us to the objective dimension of "transcendent selfhood." Being a person (*hypostasis*) vs. being an individual (*atomos*) means being a subject who possesses himself *in the act of relating one's whole being to that of another or others.* Relationship *presupposes* self-possession, yet self-possession occurs and grows *only in healthy relationships.* As John Crosby says, a human person is a "subjectivity existing in openness to a certain infinity and therefore facing an external world...in this way...[he] brings the transcendence of intentional acting into the very act of personal being."[76]

Another way of expressing this important paradox is to say that becoming a person means entering into an I-Thou relationship. In an "I-Thou" relationship, the "I" is fully developed when it is self-possessed, yet it *becomes more fully actualized* in its relationship with a "Thou." The self-possessed "I" regards the "Thou" as "totally other," acknowledging the other's own incommunicable, hypostatic goodness and beauty. The "I" never uses the "Thou" for its own, personal satisfaction. Personal satisfaction and self-fulfillment come as by-products of "treating others as I would be treated" and "loving my neighbor as myself." The "I" is in inseparable relationship with the "thou." I come to be most fully who "I am" only in a *communio personarum*.

Here again we glimpse the human analogue of the Persons within the Trinity. There is nothing "atomic" about, or in, the Trinity. To borrow a crude, chemical analogy: the structure (form) of the Trinity is inherently "molecular." The separate Persons are forever indivisible and inseparable. Similarly with human relationships that are both living and life giving: when a human "I-Thou" relationship is functioning well, it reflects the Persons of the Trinity, ever surrendered to each other in self-gifting love, their separate *Hypostases* never being confused in their act mutual giving and receiving. We can never return often enough to the Trinitarian Source of human persons-in-relation.

Let us summarize the dangers of an ego-centric (atomistic) definition of the human person. *Atomistic autonomy* destroys the possibility of *theonomous ecstasy* for the human person in a way opposite from the repression of the person by *totalistic heteronomy*. Whereas heteronomy reduces the person to a disposable element in larger impersonal whole, atomism isolates the person from mutual, life-giving relationships. It deprives a person from life with and for others and turns him into a self-seeking individual. It eliminates the polarity of any "I-Thou" relationships in favor of an "I" lacking in self-possession, self-mastery,

---

[76] Crosby, *Selfhood of the Human Person,* 173.

and self-restraint. Instead of affirming the "transcendent" selfhood of the human person, isolated individualism reinforces the "immanentism" of the personal ego. It reduces *eros* from a holy "reaching out to another" into a narcissistic "grasping the other" for my own satisfaction. It short-circuits the intentionality of the human person. It turns passionate desire into craven self-seeking. It turns the self's focus from the beauty and goodness of the world back onto itself, not for the purpose of self-examination, self-mastery, or self-evaluation, but for ends of self-gratification and self-exultation.

The problem with atomism is not the "self" *per se*, but the act of the self limiting the self to the self. Just as Buddhism and Hinduism de-personalize human persons when they seek to overcome the self by dissolving the self, radical autonomy de-personalizes the *imago Dei* when it isolates the self by *exalting* the self. Neither the monistic or pantheistic systems of heteronomy nor the atomistic or idiopathic exultation of the autonomous individual do justice to the singular mystery of the human person. Only the beautiful Person of Jesus Christ, perfect in indissoluble yet unconfused communion with the Father and the Holy Spirit, offers the model and the means for the achievement of true human personhood.

*Section Two*

# *Communio*

# EK-STATIC PERSONHOOD:
# BEYOND ATOMOS

*I*f a person (*hypostasis*) is always more than an isolated individual (*atomos*) and always more mysterious than a humanized instance of a preceding essence or substance (*ousia*), we must now explore in more detail what makes possible this "always more." The person is never a monad, despite the triumph of *hypostasis* which affirms the priority of the person as an incommunicable mystery in and of himself.

It is *relationship* (belonging, *communio*) that makes a person fully a person. The fullness of personhood is realized, actualized, and "brought into being," through communication and communion with others. *Full, mature personhood is constituted by communion.* To be a person is to be in living, loving relationships with others. Apart from such relationships, a person can be said not to be fully alive and, in a certain sense, not even to "exist."

Radical statements like these hearken back to our reflections on the Triune God. The priority of Person over Substance in God is imaged forth in everything we observe about human persons-in-relation. As *imago Dei*, human persons reflect and participate in the *ontologically relational* nature of the Three Person God. Just as the Persons in the Godhead are forever unconfused, yet forever inseparable, so too are human persons truly human only when entering with full self-possession into unconditionally committed relationships. A person's sense of self grows, intensifies, and is made complete, only in self-giving relations with others.

Other paradoxical mysteries we saw in connection with the Trinitarian *Communio Personarum* also inform our reflections on human personhood. Just as "being" and "relationship" are eternally simultaneous within the Trinity, communion and personal identity are likewise simultaneous for the human person. I have "personal" being and personal "existence," only in so far as I know and discover myself in relation with others. Just as the "otherness" of the Persons of the Trinity never precedes their eternal "togetherness," neither does the unique identity of the human person ever "come to be" except in face-to-face encounters with others. A person's "otherness," or uniqueness, actually emerges and is firmly established only in intimate connection with another. Otherwise the self flies off into isolation narcissistically locked into a neurotic or even psychotic configuration of terminal atomism.

The philosophy of the Enlightenment is rightly indicted for perverting the "triumph of *hypostasis* (personhood) into the victory of the "transcendental ego." Descartes' *Meditations* and Kant's *Critiques of Pure and Practical Knowledge* are viewed fountainhead examples of what has been called the "Copernican Revolution" in philosophy. Figures like Rousseau, Descartes, and Kant are often quoted to show how, philosophically speaking, the human subject has become the "sun" around which the world now revolves. This revolution views the human mind as both the limit and measure of knowable truth. Human subjectivity, especially cognition, is seen as an Archimedean fulcrum upon which all human knowing rests. Radically independent of external reality, the human subject is presumed to be equipped and competent to make all the critical judgments necessary to create a better life in this world.

Radical individualism and social utopianism quickly emerge from this victory of the isolated ego of Enlightenment philosophy. For Enlightenment thinkers, community is nothing other than an arbitrary social contract (Hobbes). It is the "noble savage" (Rousseau), fully free in an imagined "state of nature," rather than the human person defined and fulfilled by his role in the social *polis* (Aristotle), that becomes the model of the ideal human being. Other human beings are viewed as threats to the liberated individual (*atomos*). Relationship and commitment are perceived to be compromises of personal independence. Freedom is seen as liberation from social and religious encumbrances represented by dogma, rules, roles, and expectations. Freedom is always defined as *freedom from* obedience, service, and authority, and as *freedom for* self-indulgence, self-interest, and self-preservation.

Society too is viewed as a "brave new world" (Huxley). Anything is possible. God can be remade in man's image and likeness (Feuerbach), and society itself can be shaped, planned, and crafted into the Kingdom of God on earth (Engels, Marx). Social engineering becomes the measure of civic responsibility. Dependence on the state – or worse, total control by the state - becomes the underbelly of enlightened minds promoting what "they know is best" for the "good of the masses." A kind of Gnostic Utopia develops in which centralized social planners, freed from all mores of natural law and any organic sense of the common good, set about reinventing society according to their distinctively subjective sense of "creating a better world." One World Order is dreamily imagined by those believe they have been prophetically enlightened to introduce into history what all previous generations were too ignorant to understand. Social Utopianism is inevitable when Trinitarian *Communio* goes into eclipse.

What becomes of love in this extrication of the self from the entanglements of society and relationship? Love becomes impossible. The "I" and the "Thou" cannot be reciprocally united in love. Love devolves into suspicious self-interest. Other persons appear as objects to satisfy my subjective needs, ideas, and desires. Love of self, defined as the development of the independent ego, is seen as "the natural state of man." There is no time or space for the Golden Rule. Trust becomes a lie. Lies become the truth. Cynicism replaces sincerity as the social lubricant. Other persons pose a threat to my self-indulgence and self-actualization. Other people become "things" that I inspect, determining whether they can be useful to me or not (utilitarianism). I regard them with caution and curiosity, assessing whether or not they can help or hurt me. Their value consists in their function. Genuine reciprocity with others is impossible. The transcendental ego is isolated and imprisoned within human subjectivity. Empathy and real connection with other people cannot occur. In the most extreme cases, "hell is other people" (Sartre).

There are, however, in Sartre, Rousseau, and the other "masters of suspicion," traces of an alternative vision. Even though Sartre, for example, says "hell is other people," his analysis of the typical human encounter provides an important clue about the real role of true subjectivity in one's experience of the other (Thou). In Sartre's description of how we experience the "the look" of another, i.e. of somebody "looking at" me, we witness a reversal of the fundamental principle of how we "see" others as objects. Normally when we "look" at persons we see them as things. *But when we find ourselves being looked at by them, we suddenly see them differently.* We are arrested by their gaze. We are caught up short. Suddenly, we see them as genuinely "other," i.e., as persons like ourselves. We experience them looking at us the way we may have otherwise been looking at them. They instantly become "other" for me. They become more "real." They appear as persons with whom I could possibly have an empathetic relationship.

This experience of the other *as other* occurs, then, only at that crucial moment *when I am seen by the other.* Paradoxically, it is when I experience myself as "being looked at" by another that I truly "see" the other as another "person." Notice, too, that in this experience of "being seen," I come to a new and different awareness of myself. It's as if I see myself in a different light *because somebody sees me.* "In the look of the other, it is not only the other who is given to me, but in the most paradoxical way, [my] very own self becomes apparent."[77]

Two simpler examples may help make this important point clear. First, let us examine the experience of looking at an icon.[78] When I look at an icon, behold, I find someone(s) already looking at me! My natural, unreflective consciousness that looks out upon another person as a "thing" is suddenly arrested when I notice that the icon has already fixed its gaze on me. My natural intentionality that regards objects as somehow subject to my own ego, is almost automatically turned

---

[77] John Panteleimon Manoussakis, *God After Metaphysics* (Bloomington: Indiana University Press, 2007) 21.

[78] Here I summarize Manoussakis' explanation of Jean-Luc Marion's understanding of the icon, *Ibid.*, 22-23.

back upon itself when I become aware of the gaze of this "other." My perception both of the other and of my self is altered by the realization that the person(s) imaged forth in the icon has seen me even before I have looked upon him. It is His gaze that first addresses me, not mine that is turned on Him. My "seeing" has turned into a "being seen." The icon resists and denies my claim to turn it into an object for my eyes. It is *I* who am made to feel that I appear before the icon, not vice versa. My sense of self in "reconstituted," as it were, in the encounter with the piercing gaze of a beautiful icon.

A similar, and perhaps deeper, analogy for the self being "constituted" by the loving gaze of another is the image of the loving mother gazing into the face of her newborn child. This is a picture employed frequently by Balthasar to disclose the inherently relational nature of personal being.[79] In one sense, the mother's child already is a fully given *hypostasis*. Every baby in embryo is truly a person and worthy of the dignity accorded every *imago Dei*. On the other hand, the child *discovers itself* in communion with the mother, specifically in light of the mother's smile. In a certain sense it is *only* in light of the mother's beneficent *prosopon* (face) that the child "comes into its first possession of itself."

The *fullness* of personhood remains only a potential reality for many human persons, since the realization of God's plan for a person's life – one's true identity – cannot occur in solitude. Our complete identity is not given, whole and entire, at the moment of conception or birth. Only in *relationships of intimate communion* – such as the child enjoys in his mother's arms gazing at her smiling eyes – can any "I" come *fully* alive. In a relationship of loving communion with a "Thou," an "I" becomes not only self-aware of itself but also grows into a mature person capable of responsible and fulfilling self-surrender.

We must envision every human person as a mystery far exceeding

---

[79] Hans Urs von Balthasar, *Explorations in Theology: Volume 3, Creator Spirit* (San Francisco: Ignatius Press, 1993) 13ff.; *Love Alone Is Credible* (San Francisco: Ignatius Press, 2004) 61-62; *Unless You Become Like This Child* (San Francisco: Ignatius Press, 1991) 17-18.

the caricature of person as *atomos*. We must appreciate the fact that every human person is an *ek-static* mystery longing to establish *schesis* (communion) with another. Conversely, we must also begin to see that *koinonia* (communion) is the precondition for every human *hypostasis* to achieve full personhood. The fullness of personhood happens for us only over time through participation in loving relationships. These life-giving relationships begin in our mother's womb and arms, and develop over a life span of interacting and communing with others.

In this process of encounter and development, we acquire "sequentially" what the Trinity enjoys naturally and eternally: true personhood. We become "by participation" what God is "by nature": persons-in-relation. The freedom, alterity, and uniqueness of the human *hypostasis* "actualize" themselves in the love, communion, and intimacy of committed relationships with others. Relationship *constitutes* human persons in a way analogous to the way the Persons in the Trinity are "constituted" by their relations among themselves. Persons-in-relation are indivisible but unconfused, undivided but forever unmixed.

# COMMUNION DIFFERENTIATES

*E*very person (*hypostasis*) is an *ek-stasis* whose true identity emerges through relationship (*schesis*). The more deeply I encounter others in intimate communion (*koinonia*) the more I discover the mysterious "who" God created me to be. Communion differentiates. Divine communion differentiates perfectly. I become more **who** I am only in loving communion with God and with others.

There are several ways in which the *ekstasis* of human personhood, driving us to self-discovery and self-fulfillment in life-giving relationships, can go awry. We will examine some of these in a moment to illustrate the paradox of personal identity being enhanced, not diminished, through *sobornost* (communion) with others. First, though, a few further reflections on the *inherent relationality* of the incommunicable *hypostasis*.

Though created utterly unique and irreplaceable by God, each human person is *ordered towards* communion with others. *Relationality* is inscribed in our very being. Even the physicality of our bodies, as Pope John Paul II reminds us, reveals that the human person, male and female, is created for union. The marital act, if we have eyes to see, is a sacramental icon of the divine plan. Nuptial union is a visible 'showing forth,' not only of Christ's love of the Church, but of God's eternal plan for all men and women to re-enter the "original unity" *(communio)* our first parents enjoyed with Him, and with each other, before the Fall. The one flesh union of man and woman in the mystery of marriage is an image of the Trinity itself. We are 'hard-wired' by God for connection and intimacy with others as a direct result of being made in the image and likeness of the divine *Communio Personarum*.

Another way of imagining our inherent orientation to differentiating union is to think of ourselves as 'hypostatic hungers' or 'human thirsts.'[80] Desire (*eros*) for union percolates at the core of our very minds, hearts, bodies and souls. Created in the image and likeness of the Triune God, we instinctively desire communion with others. This desire is, in turn, both a reflection and means of achieving communion with that same Tri-personal God. Just as God Himself is an *ek-static* Communio of union-seeking Divine *Hypostases*, we too are made to image forth and participate in *ek-static* communions that both symbolize and share in the Trinitarian *ek-stasis*.

Our élan for *mutuality*, therefore, is *essential* to our nature (being) as human persons. Our "need" for communion is not an accidental or secondary 'quality,' 'added on' to our uniqueness as separate and incommunicable *hypostases*. It is *constitutive* of our very personhood. In other words, I am not *completely* myself until I am united in self-possessed communion with others.

Seen from this perspective, other persons are never threats to 'my individuality.' They are divinely offered 'gifts,' calling and attracting me into forms of communion that fulfill me as a person and contribute to Jesus' mission "for the life of the world." "I" can truly "ex-ist" only so long as I can relate to a "Thou" who affirms my existence and my "otherness" (uniqueness). My hypostatic identity is 'brought home' to me, as it were, only in respectful relationship (*koinonia*) with others. Isolated from a 'thou,' I lose touch with who 'I' really am.

Just as the Father cannot be conceived as for even an instant 'without the Son and Spirit,' neither can I be fully the person I am in God's Trinitarian vision for me separated from relationships with others. My *need for others* reflects the inseparability of the Trinitarian Communion. The freedom I enjoy as a unique and irreplaceable *hypostasis* is never *freedom from* others but always *freedom for* intimacy and communion with them. To be perfectly fruitful and fulfilled as the "who" God created me to be, my relationships must image forth and draw their life from the Trinitarian *Communio*. They must reflect and participate in the

---

[80] A phrase borrowed from Thomas Dubay, S.M., ...*And You are Christ's: The Charism of Virginity and the Celibate Life* (San Francisco: Ignatius Press, 1987) 21.

perfect "otherness-in-communion and communion-in-otherness" that constitutes the life of the Trinity.

There are more than a few ways in which this Trinitarian ideal for human relationships can fail to materialize. "Heteropathic identification," John Crosby tells us, is one such way.[81] A more common, current term for this particular distortion is "codependence." Both phrases describe how the God-given desire for communion can degenerate into slavish and self-destructive merging. Unity, within a truly personalist perspective, is never uniformity. Communion is never absorption. True togetherness always *enhances* alterity (otherness, uniqueness), never diminishes it. *True communion differentiates*, whereas codependence always debilitates. In codependent relationships, what is intended to fulfill difference-in-unity (communion) ends up by submerging the person in an undifferentiated sea of chaos. Attempts at intimacy, which are meant to unify and clarify the living freedoms of the persons engaged, quickly decompose into an unhealthy identification in which the two persons 'blend' in to each other in unhealthy and spiritually deadening ways. Mothering becomes smothering. Symbiosis becomes suffocation. Synergy becomes submission.

Heteropathic identification or codependence represents the flip side of the opposite distortion of *communio* discussed above, i.e., "radical autonomy." Just as living as an *atomos* is a mistaken attempt to affirm the singularity of the *hypostasis* (person) by pitting the 'self' against 'others,' codependence perverts true communion by mixing and dissolving what is meant to remain separate and distinct. *Atomos* separates what God has united; codependence unites what God has made to remain uniquely separate.

Both distortions of *communio* stem ultimately from 'the reign of sin in our members' (Rom. 7:23). Our capacity to perceive the Trinitarian brilliance that reveals and illumines the pattern for life-giving relationships flowing from the Trinitarian *Communio Personarum* is darkened by the effects of Original Sin and by our own actual sins. Because of the Fall, we are naturally inclined to see both the uniqueness

---

[81] Crosby, *Selfhood of the Human Person*, 107.

of human persons and our desire for union in ways *un*illumined by the Trinitarian Mystery. We attempt to define the human person in biological, psychological, sociological, and political terms, often without insight into the real workings of the human heart or the deep-down beauty and truth of human relationships. We are like the blind men whom Jesus begins to heal in the gospel: "We see people but they look like trees" (Mk. 8:24). With St. Paul we realize that we 'see through a glass darkly" (1 Cor. 13:12). Only through deep conversion, frequent reception of the sacraments, and on-going contemplative (mystical) prayer can we be brought to a place where we see relationships, and the in-built human desire for union with others, as fully illumined by the resplendent light of Jesus Christ.

Another way of stating our situation is to say we must *ascend* to the Trinity if we wish to acquire a vision of *koinonia* as God intends it to be lived out on earth. The sin of Adam and Eve causes us to misinterpret the divinely *ek-static* character of the human person. We mistake the image for the reality, the icon for the archetype. Love becomes lust. Compassion becomes control. "Seeking union" deteriorates into "seeking possession of." *Eros* is co-opted as eroticism. Our "élan for mutuality" becomes a "craving for control." Elements of covetedness enter every equation, perverting the mystery of relationality the Trinity intended for us by creating us as images of Father, Son, and Holy Spirit. The beautiful instinct of being "oriented towards" another degenerates into "seeking after" others for self-gratification.

This tragedy is complete once the *ek-static* impulse has glommed on to what it desires. *Communio* becomes a mish-mash of blurred boundaries and syrupy selves mixed together to produce an unpalatable gruel. Desperate for 'erotic communion,' persons compromise and surrender their own sense of 'who' they are in order to 'make the relationship work.' Codependence masquerades as genuine *communio*. One's 'self' is sacrificed to 'my significant other' in order to preserve a relationship of mutual manipulation. Those trapped in such "heteropathic identification" are inextricably interlocked with each other, but it is not a union that 'differentiates and clarifies.' It is a parasitic arrangement in which two persons who do not know themselves very well are trying to make 1+1=3. Sadly, such persons have entered into a 'blended' relationship that mocks real communion. Their God-given 'desire for union' has, under the influence of sin, been twisted into a 'craving for companionship.' The inevitable result is an unhealthy symbiosis that proves destructive of the persons enmeshed within it.

The spiritual implications of this morass are substantial. The devil can use anything for his purposes. Doesn't it stand to reason that he would seek to pervert – to twist, mock, deface, and mar – those very desires and instincts God has given us for *communio* that defines our existence as His *imago Dei*? Ever seeking to ruin the re-creative work of God, The Evil One works day and night to distort the nuptial meaning of the body. Within the culture of death he has created, and using the hermeneutic of suspicion he has employed as "a liar and murderer from the beginning" (Jn. 8:44), he succeeds in presenting the nuptial union in ways that take us away from God and prevent intimate *communio* with Him. He takes the most sacred icon of Trinitarian love and Christ's union with His Church – the one flesh union of man and woman – and uses this beautiful mystery of communion as his primary instrument of division and destruction. Instead of seeing the marital act as the sacrament of commitment and fidelity it was created to be, we fall prey to the influence of the world, the flesh, and the devil, and we experience as concupiscent what in truth is sacred.

We must return, therefore, to a contemplative reflection on the Persons of the Trinity, as our best way of mitigating the mind-numbing effects of the evil one's lies. Just as the Persons of the Trinity "exist" "without confusion" and "without division," so also are human persons "inherently incommunicable" (separate and unique), as well as "meant for union." We are neither "radically autonomous" (*atomos*) nor "codependently connected." Just as freedom and love, otherness and communion, are perfectly united and mutually defining within the Trinity, so the relationships existing between and among human persons are meant to be co-enhancing and mutually perfecting. "Others" are not naturally enemies of mine, nor are they mere objects intended for my use or disposal. Rather, such persons are "gifts" given me by God to assist me on my journey towards union with Him. I discover both God and myself by entering into *sobornost* (communion) with those with whom God has gifted. *Sobornost, koinonia, communio, union*: these are not ideals calling for the sacrifice of the self in codependent surrender; instead, they are images of the perfection of selfhood in which I am drawn out of myself to encounter others in mutually-enriching relationship. Authentic relationships with others always result in greater self-possession and interior freedom, thus enabling a more mature and truly "personal" self-surrender.

Difficulty getting familiar and comfortable with such odd-sounding, elliptical descriptions is a result of Original Sin, as well as poor catechesis. Many modern Christians are unacquainted with the patristic tradition that continually contemplated the Trinitarian Mystery. We are unfamiliar with the key Christological affirmations such as "There never was a time when the Son was not," or "The Father, Son, and Spirit are never without each other." These double negatives, and other such untoward phrases, were crafted by the early Church Fathers to point to the transcendent and paradoxical Mystery of Trinitarian truth. Today, many have little idea of the significance of these ancient formulae of our faith.

The answer, as always, is to return to the sources: not simply to the historical sources of the ancient Christian writers, but to the Wellspring of Worship itself, the Triune God as apprehended in contemplative prayer. As we learn how to move back and forth between the polarities involved in contemplating the Hypostatic Union, we eventually find ourselves, through prayer, gaining a sense of the difference-in-unity within the Trinity that illumines human relationships. We experience Father, Son, and Holy Spirit as the primordial Mystery shedding His light upon the truth and meaning of human love. We experience the Trinity as revealing to us that human love worthy of God always "lifts and separates," never "submerges and conflates." We see clearly that "union differentiates" and differences among persons are perfected only in communion.

# HIERARCHICAL AND ESCHATOLOGICAL COMMUNIO

*T*he *ek-static communio (koinonia, schesis)* that constitutes and perfects the human *hypostasis* (person) has two further dimensions that complete what has gone before. These additions also anticipate what is yet to come. For *communio* truly reflective of the Trinitarian Mystery is also both hierarchical and eschatological. Jesus is both Alpha and Omega, the Beginning and the End. The Eternal Word is present at the beginning of the world as its Creator and present at its consummation as its Lord and Savior. Christ is forever working both ends of human existence, drawing all persons back into Original Unity with His Father. He is present not just as the One who "makes possible" human *koinonia,* but also as the One who "gathers all things to Himself" (Jn. 12:32). He is the Originator and Finisher of all that is. All that the Father has is His, and everything that He has He gives to His Father (Jn. 6:39). His mission is to deliver back to the Father all that was lost through the sin of Adam and Eve.

The freedom that Christ and the Holy Spirit enjoy within the Trinity must be distinguished from that of the Father. The Son and the Spirit are "begotten" of the Father. God the Father is not "begotten" of them. The Son and the Spirit "proceed from" the Father, not vice versa. As noted above, the Father enjoys a *"monarchia"* within the Trinity that is not given to Son and Spirit. Thus there exists a "hierarchical" relationship within the Trinity, from which flow and derive other asymmetrical relationships we encounter in the world of human persons.

The "priority of the Father" within the Trinitarian *Communio* does not imply or necessarily lead to the various forms of subordinationism that marked the heresies of the early church. Those the Church declared heretics could not, or would not, grasp the idea that the "hierarchy" within the Trinity does not involve inequality or diminishment in dignity of either the Son or the Spirit. Within the Trinity the Father is "always greater" than the Son and the Spirit (cf. Jn. 14:28). He "generates" the Son, and the Holy Spirit "proceeds" from Him. Nevertheless, both Son and Holy Spirit enjoy full and equal ontological status with the Father as God. The Father is as much "surrendered" to them as they are to Him, though the forms of their mutual service reveal and express the distinctiveness of each of the separate Persons of the Trinity.

What does this intra-Trinitarian divine 'causality' reveal to us about the nature of *human* relationships? Just as personal 'otherness' within the Trinity is a-symmetrical, there are elements of a-symmetry and apparent inequality inherent in all human relationships as well. This is something to be expected, even desired, not something to shunned or avoided. Men and women, for example, are created equal in dignity but are different in almost every other way. Within the nuptial mystery of marriage, which reflects both the Trinitarian *Communio* and Christ's Headship in His Church (Eph. 5:23), the man is "head of the woman" (1Cor. 11:7-9; Eph. 5:23). This implies absolutely no loss of dignity for woman or any special privilege for man. Only a "hermeneutic of suspicion," fueled by a fallen, non-Trinitarian vision of the human person, implies otherwise. Children, too, are expected to be *obedient* to their parents (Eph. 6:1). This is not because parents are somehow ontologically superior to their children, but because certain roles are ordained by the Triune God, whose own immanent Trinitarian Life is the divine wellspring of all such differences and distinctions.

This hierarchical ordering of all personal relations presupposes and complements the *transcendent* nature of human selfhood. Human personhood, as we have seen, is inherently *ek-static*, i.e., it depends for its fulfillment on intimate and committed involvements with others. Human persons are never self-existent or self-explicable. They must be 'brought into (full) being' through communion with an 'other'. These 'others' must be seen as God's gifts to me. They 'perfect' and 'complete' me as a person. I experience them as persons who are 'prior' and, in some sense, always 'greater' than me. I can only 'receive' their friendship and 'come to full stature' within it. All friendship "draws me up into itself." My desire for communion fulfills itself in committed relationships with others. This involves me in various roles, inequalities, and asymmetrical dynamics within several, many-layered relationships with others.

This returns us to Jesus as the Alpha and Omega. He is the divine "Other" who seeks to assimilate us to Himself and to return us to His Father. The "truth" of our deepest personal identity is found ultimately only in God Himself, i.e., in relationship with the Persons of the Trinity. In heaven, God reveals to us 'the white stone' on which is written our true name (Rev. 2:17). This is our primordial identity within the life of the Trinity. This is the person God created me to be from all eternity. My identity is fully disclosed to me only at the end of my journey. Christ is the Omega who reveals to me at the End, who He created me at the Beginning, and who has known me 'from before the foundation of the world' (Eph. 1:9). The truth of things, then – both for me, personally, and for the world, generally – lies more in the *future* than in the present. My true identity is 'manifest' to some extent through my life-giving relationships in the present, but is fully disclosed only at the end. When contemplating our life in the Trinity, we must always begin with the End in mind.

The same can be said about the 'truth' of creation. Both nature and history are oriented towards Christ the Omega. Perfection is not an original state of nature to which creation or history automatically returns. On the contrary, perfection is goal (*telos*) which is even now being brought to completion by the One who is 'yet to come." It is the Second Coming of Christ that completes and fulfills the Redemption and Salvation that His Paschal Mystery has already achieved. Paradoxically, *the truth of history lies in the future*. Human history is not simply a movement *towards* an end; it is more truly a movement *from* the End. We are involved in a Theo-drama[82] in which the Final Act has yet to appear.

As the Omega Point, Jesus pulls history forward from his position at the right hand of the Father (Eph. 1:20). Those who live "in Christ" are already seated with Him in glory at the right hand of the Father (Eph. 2:6). We live with Him and reign with Him, even in our present life. At the same time, the narrative quality of our own experience allows us to share in the suffering and death of His Paschal Mystery. The meaning of history *is* the life, death, resurrection, and ascension of Jesus. Though a once-only series of genuinely historical events, the Incarnation and sacrifice of Christ lives on forever. It functions as the *telos* of human history, exercising a divinely magnetic pull on the ebbs and flows, cross-currents and eruptions, of history. Not for an instant does it interrupt, discount, or cancel the smallest exercise of human freedom. Yet, it incorporates all actions, choices, and decisions of human persons into the transcendental Theo-drama centralized in the Passion of Christ. The "truth of history": has appeared in the actions, words, and events of the life of Christ. In His ascended glory, Jesus, the Son of God and the Son of Man is still 'pulling history forward' through the power of the Holy Spirit. He is "bringing to completion" His divine Plan of salvation in ways a-symmetrical with the schemes and systems human persons. The 'truth' of history is Jesus Himself. "I am the Way, the Truth, and the Life," He says (John 14:6). He is also the Omega (Rev. 1:8). "When I am lifted up, I will draw all men to myself" (Jn. 12:32). At the beginning and end of history, Jesus is present, drawing all persons into communion with Himself, in faithful obedience to the Father.

There is also a cosmological dimension to Jesus as "the Way, the Truth, and the Life." In Him, all of *creation*, not just human persons, finds its ultimate "truth" and "being" (Rom. 8). Personal truth and

---

[82] The term used by Hans Urs von Balthasar to describe the intersections of the "Two Freedoms" of God and man in dramatic, eschatological terms. See his, *Theo-Drama: Theological Dramatic Theory, Volume II* (hereafter TD, II), Dramatis Personae: Man in God, trans. Graham Harrison (San Francisco: Ignatius Press, 1990) 173-316.

the truth of nature can no longer be separated. There is no such thing as the 'truth of human persons' separated from the 'truth of history' or even from the 'truth of natural science.' Nor can the natural or social sciences be divorced from "the truth about the human person." As Pope Benedict XVI has stated, "The whole draws its meaning from the individual, not the other way around...The all-encompassing 'complexification', the unification infinitely embracing all, is at the same time the denial of all collectivism, the denial of the fanaticism of the mere idea, even the so-called 'idea of Christianity.' Man, the person, always takes precedence over the mere idea."[83] This is because Truth is ultimately a Person, the Person of Jesus. In Him, "we live and move and have our being" (Acts 17:28). Everything is brought to completion only "in Christ".

History and creation be rightly understood only when all things are seen to derive their existence and meaning from Jesus, the *Christus Totus.*. The meaning and purpose, indeed the very 'being,' of all things created are found only "in Christ." The meaning of created being and the purpose of history *are* the incarnate Christ. This is why the patristic tradition insisted so strongly that the Incarnation would have occurred irrespective of the fall of man.[84] Christ, the incarnate God, is forever the Truth. In his flesh, He is the ecstatic love of God, leading all of created being into communion with His own Trinitarian life. Before and after the Fall, the meaning of human life is to know Jesus within His communion with the Father and the Holy Spirit. We are created for the purpose of being "in Christ." It is not just Adam's sin that created our need for Jesus. To "exist" is to be created and oriented to fulfillment only "in Christ." In order to "fully alive" we must be assimilated into Him in an eschatological fullness that not only "completes" us, but also, in some sense, enables Christ Himself to "come to full stature" (Eph, 1:23; 2:22; 4:15).

This vision of Jesus as Truth allows us to begin to see how important

---

[83] Pope Benedict XVI, *Credo for Today: What Christians Believe* (San Francisco: Ignatius Press, 2009) 115.

[84] John Zizioulas, *Being as Communion: Studies in Personhood and the Church,* 97, n. 89.

both creation and human persons are to God. We are, in some sense, "necessary" to His very identity as God. All things were created with Christ in mind. "In Christ," we constitute with Him the Total Christ (*Christus Totus*). The "Mystical Body" of Christ, as we have seen, is no mere metaphor. It is a divine, transcendent mystery in which human persons and all of creation form an integral part. "The Lord takes delight in His people" (Ps. 149) is not simply a pious cliché. The affectivity attributed to God throughout the Scripture cannot be written off as tawdry sentimentality or unenlightened anthropocentrism. It reveals a certain kind of "receptivity" within the life of the Trinity itself. This receptivity includes the incorporation of created reality into the very life of God.

There is a real sense in which God "needs" and "delights" in our freely-given response to His invitation of love. He "thrills" to our dialogue and communion with Him. He "has need of us" (cf. Mt. 21:3) in ways that neither threaten nor diminish His immutability.[85] His desire for union with us is not secondary to His nature as a Tri-Personal God.

The idea that God "needs" or "desires" all of creation, especially human persons, to "complete" Him sounds suspicious to a theology that lacks the priority of *hypostasis*. The "receptivity" and "desire for union" inscribed into the very being of human *ek-stasis* must find a counterpart in God if the reality of "God in search of man"[86] is not to degenerate into panentheism or some other form of New Age Gnosticism. Both we and the world are "needed and wanted" by God, but not in ways that threaten God's aseity or cause God to "suffer."[87]

---

[85] On the immutability of God amidst His desire that we be incorporated into Him through Jesus, see G.F. O'Hanlon, S.J., *The Immutability of God in the Theology of Hans Urs von Balthasar* (New York: Cambridge University Press, 1990).

[86] This mystically Christian concept finds a beautiful Jewish affirmation in the work of Abraham Joshua Heschel, *Man in Search of God*, (New York: Farrar, Straus and Giroux, 1985).

[87] For the importance of always 'protecting' the aseity of God, notwithstanding the sense being developed here of God "needing" us, see Thomas G. Weinandy, O.F.M., Cap., *Does God Suffer?*, (Notre Dame, IN: University of Notre Dame Press) 200..

The early church fathers used the idea of "participation" (*methexis*) in God to describe the link between Jesus, the Logos, and the things (*logoi*) of world. As we will discuss in more detail later, the notion of "participation" enabled the Fathers to affirm the communion of God and the world in a way that protects the transcendence of God and secures the natural integrity of things. Creatures "participate" in God; God never "participates" in creation. The 'truth' of creation is a *dependent* truth, while the truth of God is independent of what He has created. Still, God creates the whole world to be "in communion" with Himself. He desires union with us in a way that parallels His own nature as a *Communio Personarum* of coinherent *Hypostases*.

Recall that the "being" of God and the world are never "univocal." God and the world cannot be placed on an ontological par with each other. The must not be seen as side by side identities, equal in being and indifferent to each other. The relative autonomy of the world is guaranteed only by being rooted in its eschatological incorporation into Christ. Similarly, the hypostatic identity of Christ includes, as vital to His mystical fullness, the whole of humankind and creation. "The distinctive integrity of creation and its union with the divine are reciprocally conditioning poles of one and the same mystery."[88]

"Jesus has need of you!" It takes us a lifetime to grasp, or be grasped, by the contemplative truth contained in this affirmation. Such a phrase flies in the face of a vision of Christianity in which the self is seen as needing to be "sacrificed" in obedience to Christ. Nor will it be appreciated by those who think "following Jesus" means simply "imitating Christ" or merely being "faithful to His moral teachings." There is infinitely more to our "incorporation into Christ" than living out the "imitation" of Christ. "Jesus has need of you!"

This proclamation has a mystical significance that transcends all utilitarian overtones. It stems from and returns to the Trinitarian *perichoresis*. Jesus created us by Himself and for Himself. We come from

---

[88] Adrian Walker, cited in Nicholas J. Healy, *The Eschatology of Hans Urs von Balthasar: Being as Communion* (Oxford: Oxford University Press: Theological Monographs, 2007) 22, n. 11.

God and return to God. We are not automatons on a cyclical journey or slaves under heteronomous obedience. On the contrary, we are free, acting persons, uniquely involved in the Theo-drama of Jesus Christ. We are participants in His "coming to full stature." The fullness of the Person of Jesus – the *Totus Christus* - includes the assimilation of us "into" Him. Though infinitely different from God by nature - always His creatures, beholden to and dependent upon Him - we are also summoned to "incorporation into" Him through the Incarnation of Jesus. Just as He is one with the Father and the Holy Spirit by nature, we become one with Him through "participation."

*Section 3*

# *Eros*

# REDEMPTION OF EROS

"*G*od created us without us," St. Augustine tells us, "but he did not will to save us without us."[89] The Tri-Personal God desires, and in some sense "needs," our freely chosen response to His invitation to communion in order to "make" His redemptive Incarnation salvific for us. A *personal* God, in other words, desires a *personal* response from the persons He has created to image forth and imitate [be icons of] His inner-Trinitarian *Communio Personarum*.

What makes for a *personal* response? More specifically, how important are *feelings* to the personal response God expects from us? For reasons too involved and complicated to go into here, subjectivity and affectivity have acquired a bad reputation in some religious circles. Especially among conservative Christians, feelings and subjective intuition seem always to be suspect. Wishing to avoid either a "touch-feely" religion or a "feel good" faith, some turn a wary eye towards those who associate interior disposition or emotional responsiveness with the holy things of faith. This is a grave mistake. *Affectivity* (emotions, feelings) is at the "heart" of the human person. "The heart has its reasons the mind knows not of" (Paschal). Our relationship with the Tri-Personal God is both intimate and *deeply affective*. It involves our emotions in a profound, integrative way. Otherwise it is essentially lacking in what makes for an enduring relationship of love with our Divine Spouse.

Let's begin by clearing the ground of some common misconceptions. First off, subjectivity is not ego-centricity. As outlined above, solidarity with one's self does not compromise charity with neighbor. On the contrary, it is the basis for a genuinely personal relationship with an

---

[89] St. Augustine, *Sermo* 169,11,13:PL 38,923, cited in CCC 1847.

"other." Respecting myself and the "other" as "other," I am able to enter into a relationship of communion that avoids the twin dangers of autonomous isolation and codependent merging. The commandment, "Love your neighbor *as yourself*" (Lev. 19:18; Mk. 12:31), reveals and validates the essential importance of self-possession and self-love in our relationships with God and others.

Despite these words of Jesus, however, many Christians persist in a negative, anemic view of personal subjectivity and human affectivity. Subjectivity is equated with "subjectivism." Affectivity is dismissed as "emotionalism." Personalism is reduced to "perspectivism," imagined to result automatically in "relativism" or a destructive kind of "pluralism." Philosophically, these are genuine menaces to authentic Christian belief. But from a personalist, Trinitarian perspective, none of these identifications are accurate. God is a Community of Persons passionately desiring to draw all human persons into unitive intimacy with Himself. This intimacy engages and transforms human affectivity in ways that are essential, not inconsequential, to the relationship He desires. The dissolution of subjectivity – which, as we noted above, is the ideal of Buddhism and Hinduism – annihilates the human person and is therefore *anathema* to Christian soteriology.

Perhaps this unfortunate substitution of stoicism for the beauty of Christian personalism is a predictable reaction to the various forms of hedonism and paganism we find appearing in the culture of death. Still, it is supernaturally stupid. The Trinitarian *perichoresis* is never indifferent to, or devoid of, a *divinely erotic energy*. *Perichoresis* is the term we use – purposely indefinable - to convey ecstatic love circulating ever more powerfully among and between the Persons in the Trinity. It is this same *perichoretic* love that we see manifested in the great theophanies of Old and New Testaments. From the Burning Bush in the desert (Ex. 3:4), to Moses face resplendent with the glory of YHWH (Ex. 34:35), to the Wedding Feast at Cana (Jn. 2:1ff.) or Jesus transfigured on Mt. Tabor (Mk. 9:2ff.): these epiphanies of God glory participate in and reveal the supremely *ek-static* nature of the divine *eros* within the Trinity.

Sadly, an ideal of stoic indifference has been the perennial perversion of certain versions of Christian teaching which have lost touch with a true Trinitarian vision in which the glory of God is shown forth in its resplendent majesty. Those who drink deeply of this vision find themselves, as St. Paul predicted, "transformed from glory to glory (2 Cor. 3:18).[90] There is a proper understanding of "indifference" as used by St. Ignatius of Loyola and others that can be very helpful in the spiritual life; but, defined in a rigorous, stoical manner, a studied "indifference" is the death of rich and rewarding relationships with God and others.

The human person is *inherently emotional*, not as a result of the Fall, but precisely as part of our creation as *imago Dei*. Personhood is *intrinsically subjective*, and therefore *essentially affective*. The "transcendent" nature of human selfhood does not compete with, or diminish in any way, the intrinsically *emotional* character of the human person. The fact that we recognize other persons as having objective (transcendent) value outside of and beyond ourselves, needing to be loved whether we feel like it or not, should not tempt us to pooh-pooh the importance of our emotional responses to persons and things in the world. Because they are ingredient to human subjectivity, such emotional responses actually function, when properly discerned, as the surest measure of our relationship with God. Jesus does not desire automatons in His service whose narrow definition of salvation is going to heaven by dutifully keeping the Commandments. Moralism is the mortal enemy of contemplative Catholicism. It turns the Christian life into a search for security instead a voyage in hope. Keeping the Commandments is a necessary but insufficient condition for entering the Kingdom of God.

In a more Trinitarian key and in more personalist terms, we can say that Jesus wants disciples who love Him *passionately*. For example, He chose the volatile and inconsistent Peter to head His Church (Mt. 16:18). He chose to appear to the bedeviled Mary the Magdalene soon after His Resurrection (Jn. 20:16). He praised the sinful woman who

---

[90] See Von Balthasar's critique of "Theopanism" in *The Glory of the Lord: A Theological Aesthetics, I: Seeing the Form* (San Francisco: Ignatius Press, 1982) 131ff. Von Balthasar shows how the false ideal of a stoic-like indifference has bedeviled Christianity from the very start.

washes his feet with her tears (Jn. 11:2; 12:3). At Bethany, He tells those who will listen, "Mary has chosen the better part, it will not be taken from her" (Lk. 10:42). Each of these persons was not exactly the dutiful servant, always keeping the Commandments perfectly. Yet, Jesus singles them out as saints special to Himself. Why? Because their *hearts* are in the right place, even if their behavior sometimes lagged behind.

It must also be pointed out that Jesus Himself is not unemotional when doing His Father's Will. He wept for his friend, Lazarus (John 11:35). He also wept for Jerusalem, soon to be destroyed for its refusal to recognize the time of its visitation (Lk. 19:41). Irritated and upset, He called the scribes and Pharisees "a brood of vipers" (Mt. 3:7; 12:34). In a fit of anger threw the vendors out of the temple who were desecrating His Father's house of prayer (Jn. 2:15). He cried out in desperation to His Father on the Cross (Mt. 27:46; cf. Lk. 23:46). Even this cursory view of episodes from Jesus' life reveals that a deeply heart-felt, affective love fuels the mission of the Savior. There is a divine passion always aflame within the Sacred Heart of Jesus. There is an infinite passion and *eros* welling up beneath His Passion and death on the Cross.

Jesus' strongest contemporary followers will be no less passionate in their love of Him. Subjectivity in the devoted disciple can never be too strong. It can only be crippled, withered, or disordered. One can never love too much, nor feel love too much. "Love," Scripture tells us, "is stronger than death." Should one try to place some limits on how much the human heart should feel and empathize, "they would be roundly mocked" and rightly dismissed (Song. 8:6-7). Love, by its very nature (Trinitarian, *perichoretic*), is infinite and limitless. It is "ever greater." "God is love, and he who abides in God abides in love" (1 Jn. 4:16). This love is not contained. It is ever effusive and diffusive of itself.

Now love's effulgence always registers in the senses. It is known affectively in the interiority of the human subject. "Mary pondered these things in her heart," St. Luke tells us (Lk. 2:19, 51). We know from Scripture that many disclosures God gives to us through His Spirit are "too deep for words" (Rom. 8:26). This does not mean they cannot be known. It means simply that the movements of God's Spirit within must be properly discerned. We must learn how to feel, listen to, and understand the promptings of the Spirit within the interiority of our hearts.[91] Indeed, precisely because our relationship with the Triune God is always personal, there is never a time in "knowing" God when we are not also "being known" by Him. This intimate experience of enjoying "knowledge" of God reverberates in our affectivity in ways that may be discerned, if not always logically or coherently described.

It is the experience of *joy* that most characterizes the person who is truly in love with God. Sadly, an emaciated definition of "love as will" has tended to replace a more personalist sense of "continually rejoicing in the Lord" (Phil. 3:1; Col. 16-17). Bewitched by the Kantian ideal of "duty," and the "categorical imperative" of "love as an act of the will," we have reverted to a philosophical indifference (*apatheia*) as a substitute for the Christian ideal of passionate love (*caritas*). The meaning of Christian charity has become domesticated. It has come to mean "caring for" someone I "ought" to be kind to, even though I may or may not "feel charitable" towards them. A false ideal of indifference (*amour desinteresse*) now passes as a bland alternative to the robust *ordo amoris* that characterizes passionate Christian piety.[92]

We must learn to assume an orientation towards God and others that partakes of the fervor of love as it exists within the *ek-static Communio* of the Trinity. "I am zealous with zeal for the house of the Lord," says the prophet, Elijah (1 Kg. 19:10). "Zeal for your house consumes me," says the Psalmist (Ps. 69:9; cf. Jn. 2:17). Do these sound like assertions of an indifferent Stoic? The person in love with God is never content with

---

[91] For an insightful treatment of the delicate art of learning how to read the movements of one's heart in the context of St. Ignatius of Loyola's Spiritual Exercises, see Timothy M. Gallagher, OMV, *The Discernment of Spirits: An Ignatian Guide for Everyday Living* (New York: Crossroads Publishing Co., 2005).

[92] The 'redemption of eros,' i.e., showing the complementarity and ultimate unity of eros and agape is the key thrust of Benedict XVI's first encyclical, Deus Caritas est. For an excellent treatment of this theme in the theology of Benedict XVI, see D.C. Schindler, "The Redemption of Eros: Philosophical Reflections on Benedict XVI's First Encyclical." Communio XXXIII, 3 (Fall 2006), 375-400.

simply "doing one's duty" or "carrying out one's obligations." Such a lack of integration between one's interior disposition and external acts of "charity" is not legitimated by claiming that "love is in the will" and therefore "what I am feeling" is of no moral consequence. Human affectivity is of great significance for moral and spiritual direction. It reminds us that intimacy with God and others – *communio* – ever exceeds and transcends simple 'moral' transactions. *Communio* with God and others is always greater than establishing a contract with them. Relationship is about commitment, which always exceeds simple compliance with a set of minimum requirements. The white-knuckled kindness of a disinterested Christian is a far cry from the beloved disciple reclining quietly on the breast of Jesus (Jn. 13:25).

Altruism is another bad facsimile of Christian charity. Altruism derives from a disownership of the self in an alleged attempt to affirm the other. It rests on the mistaken notion that a person best achieves his or her full destiny when they no longer considers any beneficial goods for themselves, but only when they are "caring" "dispassionately" for others. Altruism is a kind of "holy patronization" in which other persons becomes "my Christian duty," and "taking care of others" is something "I am supposed to do" in order to "achieve my salvation." Altruism de-personalizes. It is a form of Christian condescension. It makes a mockery of true Trinitarian relationality.

The same sort of altruistic instrumentalism can infect one's spiritual life as well. I can look at serving my neighbor simply as a means of "saving my soul." Keeping the Second Great Commandment ("Love they neighbor as they self") for the sole purpose of "glorifying God" or "going to heaven" is a harsh and heretical surrogate for the mystery of true Christian charity. Such spiritual utilitarianism perverts the mystery of personalist interaction. Real Christian empathy is possible only for the self-possessed person who is intimately in touch with the interior and affective movements of his or her own heart. Otherwise, what presents itself as Christian kindness is narcissism disguised as compassion and pride masquerading as benevolence. Covertly, I fancy myself a savior on a crusade to rescue "the poor" who "can't do without my assistance." The darkest forms of insolence and patronization often present themselves as the angels of light of kindness and compassion.

The false ideals of both stoicism and altruism stem from the failure to appreciate the personalist mystery of the Trinitarian *communio*. In the Trinity we discover an "ontology of relationality" that affirms difference within unity. Love circulates among the Trinitarian Persons in a manner that is anything but "indifferent." There is a *passio* at the heart of the Trinitarian Mystery that is both active and eternally unceasing. The human experience of *eros,* even in its fallen state, derives directly from this *perichoretic* ecstasy (*ek-stasis*) within the Trinity. As human persons we can never not experience others in a deeply affective manner. To seek to eliminate our affective responses in the name of some higher, more abstract ideal is to drain human relationships of the very energy that makes us images of the Trinity. In the end, all love, especially Christian love, has deeply affective and subjective dimensions. They must be owned, appreciated, and integrated into the persons we are, made in the image and likeness of God. There is nothing artificial, arbitrary, or ancillary in our affective responses to persons and things in the world. Our loves and hates appear to us as powerful emotions for a very good reason. They reflect the Trinitarian *eros,* and, if properly discerned, can draw us more deeply into it.

This is also why the mystery of the *person* of Jesus always exceeds His "message." The commandments of Christ are more a summons to intimacy than they are a super-imposed system for achieving salvation. We are not commanded or forced by Christ to enter into the Trinitarian Embrace, we are invited. Christ desires followers who experience the same longing, yearning, and desire for Him that characterize His own burning love of His Father.

Pope John Paul II calls the process of earning how to discern and appreciate the divine significance of the affective movements within us "an apprenticeship in self-mastery." He says such a process enables "acting persons" to better resemble the Divine *Communio Personarum*. Appreciation of our own subjectivity and interiority is necessary, he says, to have truly personal relations with others. In so doing, we acquire an integrated sense of what he calls the "personalist principle." This principle states that "the person is a good towards which the only proper attitude is love...[and] does not admit of use and cannot be treated as an object of use [or merely a] means to an end."[93] This love involves a full flowering of human affectivity, purified and refined through the "apprenticeship in self-mastery." It partakes of the *perichoresis* of the Trinity, that divine *passio* and transcendent *eros* that is the source of joy ever radiant in the faces of His saints.

---

[93] Wojtyla, *Love and Responsibility*, 41.

# TRIUNE SUBJECTIVITY

*R*estoring subjectivity and affectivity to their rightful, pre-Adamic state within a Christian vision of the human person is difficult because the effects of the Fall. We tend to see as divided what God intends to be united. We try to acquire through analysis what is only really apprehended through contemplative intuition.

To regain a contemplative perspective on the importance of *eros* for the spiritual life requires a lengthy process of discipline and purification. We must always return to the Trinity to acquire a true vision of the human person. Faculties within the human person that we tend to see as separate and subordinate must be re-viewed as integrated and mutually supportive in an appreciation of human subjectivity that is governed by a Trinitarian vision.

The saints have spoken of a *triune subjectivity* within the human person that mirrors the Blessed Trinity. Some have identified this triune consciousness with the image and likeness of God within us. Some have spoken less boldly of the human person as comprised of mind, body, and spirit, or of body, soul, and spirit. Still others, such as St. John of the Cross, have described human subjectivity as an integrated unity of intellect, memory, and will. In what follows we will consider *cognition (mind, intellect), volition (will, free choice), and affection (feeling, emotion)* as key components of human interiority. We will reflect on these as the form of triune consciousness within us that mirrors the mystery of the Trinity in its perfect unity-in-difference. We will also consider these faculties under their more patristic descriptions as *nous* (cognition or mind), *thymos* (volition or will), and *eros* (affection or heart). Our main concern here is the redemption of *eros:* the same project of rehabilitation that Pope Benedict XVI attempts to achieve in his encyclical, *Deus Caritas Est.* With him, we seek to restore love, especially in its affective dimensions, to its rightful place as the centerpiece of human, triune subjectivity.

We know from St. Paul that among the theological virtues, "the greatest of these is love" (1 Cor. 13:13). Love occupies among the theological virtues the same kind of *monarchia* position of priority that God the Father enjoys within the Trinity. Might not the *heart,* and its affections (*eros*), occupy a similar place within the human person? Within the western philosophical and theological traditions, the mind (intellect, *nous*) has enjoyed long-time superiority over the heart (affections, *eros*) as our primary means of knowing. But is not biblical knowledge, with its more spousal and sapiential overtones, both deeper and more personal than the intellectual pursuit of empirical certainty that our contemporary world considers the measure of truth? We believe so. Restoring *eros* (love, heart, feeling, affection, emotion) to its rightful (monarchial) place in a triune vision of human consciousness affirms the unity-in-difference of the Blessed Trinity, as well as affirms St. Paul's exhortation about the priority of love.

Central to the restoration of *eros* as the primordial way of human knowing is to see that feelings (*eros,* affections, emotions, likes and dislikes, attraction and aversion) are both omnipresent and always intentional. We are never not feeling something. Our response to people, places, situations, and other things in the world is always registering in our emotions, even if we sometimes have a difficulty identifying such emotions.

The fact that a person can be anesthetized to his or her feelings should not convince us that they are unimportant. A person can certainly deaden a sense of what they are experiencing affectively, just as a person can de-sensitize one's self to the movements of one's conscience. But neither the feelings nor the conscience cease operating simply because the person is out of touch with how these faculties are operating. Similarly, one can confuse emotions with ideas and other non-emotional movements within, just as one can confuse conscience with super-ego. But affectivity and cognition are never the same, just as conscience and super-ego cannot be conflated. Indeed, both conscience and affectivity go deeper than other aspects of our interiority with which we may be tempted to identify them. The "reasons of the heart" are known at a depth unknown to the intellect. The head is meant to be the servant to the heart, not vice versa.

The "knowledge" acquired by the affections (emotions) in the depths of the heart must not be discredited or minimized by being described as "merely subjective." Our emotions attain the truth, even if their way of communicating the truth to us differs from the way in which the intellect (*nous*) does. Affection and emotion are not only omnipresent, they are also *precisely intentional.* They reach out to, and respond to, objects (truths, goods) independent of themselves in very specific and well-defined ways. They recognize in a keen, visceral, and uncanny way, the relative value or lack of value in the objects to which they are responding. They represent our deepest, and in some sense, truest response to objects and values that exist independently of ourselves. When properly trained, purified, and deified through conversion, reception of the sacraments, and contemplative prayer, these affective responses to the objects, persons, and situations we encounter become a virtually infallible means of discerning the Will of God for our lives. Emotion (defined here as *eros*) is the ineluctable *value-response* within the human person that most deeply resembles and represents the voice of God.

These are unusual claims. In what follows I will not so much attempt to justify them as to show how, within a triune vision of human subjectivity, the priority of love (*eros*), in all its affective (emotional) dimensions, is rightly described by many of the saints as the *primary measure of truth* and the most reliable way of discerning God direction for our lives.

I mentioned earlier that we know from St. Paul that among the theological virtues of faith, hope, and love, "the greatest of these is love" (1 Cor. 13:13). Let us now connect the theological virtues – and the priority of love among them – with what are know in philosophy as the three "transcendentals": beauty, goodness, and truth. Let us further connect the virtues and transcendentals with the three dimensions of human triune subjectivity: *nous* (intellect, mind), *thymos* (will, volition), and *eros* (love, affection). We now have a triune correlation that looks something like this:

| | | | |
|---|---|---|---|
| ***Nous*** | = Faith | Intellect | Truth |
| ***Thymos*** | = Hope | Will | Goodness |
| ***Eros*** | = Love | Heart | Beauty |

In God, truth, goodness, and beauty are one. Philosophy refracts them through the prism of fallen human analysis into the three separate "transcendentals." This represents a futile attempt to grasp the nature of God through reason alone. These efforts are accurate, and can be helpful as far as they go. They become dangerous to our understanding of both God and the human person, however, when they become too compartmentalized or antagonistic to one another. When "truth," for example, is said to enjoy a priority over "goodness" and "beauty," something important about the mystery of knowledge has been lost. This results in a disintegration of the human person. Knowing and loving become separate activities. Mind and heart are divided. The will is left in abeyance. Anarchy and chaos result. Depression and despair take over.

Only a Triune vision can lead to a proper anthropology. If truth, goodness, and beauty are united in God; and if faith, hope, and charity correspond as theological virtues in us as correlates to truth, goodness, and beauty in God; and if love is the "greatest" of the theological virtues, then: might not *beauty* be the primary descriptive we should use to describe the Trinitarian Mystery? And might not love (*eros*, affectivity) be the primary means to we employ to enter into contact and communion with the beauty of the Trinity? Following Balthasar, I believe this to be the case.[94]

Entering into the beauty of God – the Glory of the Lord – is the most fruitful mode of theological reflection. It is *love* within the human heart that ultimately attains God. This love is moved most deeply by the

---

[94] *The Glory of the Lord*, Volume I (hereafter GL, I): *Seeing the Form*, 18.

*beauty* of the Lord. This love is also quite intentional in its affectivity. The intensity of human longing and satisfaction is registered in the emotions. These emotions, in turn, become our best barometer for discerning the nature and degree of our union with the Triune God.

None of this is achieved easily or quickly. A great and on-going conversion is required, both in our appreciation of affectivity and in our understanding the movements of our own hearts, in order for the restoration of *eros* as the means and measure of our relationship with God and others to occur. Yet, nothing is more worthwhile pursuing at a time when naked intellect and power have replaced heart-felt empathy as the measure of value in a culture of death. A restoration of love as the measure of truth is the needed antidote to counter act the harmful effects of the dictatorship of relativism.

Importantly, the restoration of *eros* is not the revival or eroticism, any more than appreciation of human subjectivity is a reversion to subjectivism or solipsism. "Our hearts are restless," says St. Augustine, "until they rest in Thee." The desire for God (*eros*) is the fundamental urge of every human person. As mentioned earlier, we are "human thirsts." We hunger and thirst for the living God. "Like the deer longs for running streams, so my soul longs for You, my God" (Ps. 42:4). Or, as the *Catechism of the Catholic Church* (#27) says, "The desire for God is written in the human heart because man is created by God and for God; and God never ceases to draw man to himself." Importantly, this desire (*eros*) is insatiable. And though it often gets projected on objects other than God, thus perverting itself into hedonism, self-indulgence, impulsiveness, inertia, and indolence, *eros* never loses its character as a divine gift ever erupting within the human person.

What then, is *eros*? *Eros*, simply defined, is the heart-felt desire for communion with another. It is a "reaching out" and a "going out unto." Human personhood, as we said at the outset, is "transcendent" personhood. The hungering self experiences completion only in communion, a communion that both fulfills and perfects the uniqueness of the singular *hypostasis* (person) who experiences this infinite and insatiable desire. *Eros* is the name of this project. *Eros* is a participation in the very life of God Who Is *Eros* (Love). "God is love, and he who abides in love, abides in God" (1 Jn. 416). Abiding in God is abiding in *Eros*. *Eros* is that goal-directed (intentional) attraction that constitutes within us the very *imago* of the *Dei* who created us. In experiencing *Eros*, we experience a taste of the mutual attraction and unquenchable "being for" and "moving towards" that obtains within the *perichoresis* of the Trinity.

*Eros* (heart, affection) finds its fulfillment in *communio* (*sobornost*, *koinonia*), just as *thymos* (will, volition) finds fulfillment in *kenosis* (humility, surrender) and *nous* (mind, cognition) finds fulfillment in *hesychasm* (purity of heart).[95] Affection, volition, and cognition form an integrated triune unity in the subjectivity of the saint. This integration reflects the perfect unity-in-difference within the Trinity. This unity is not quickly achieved. *Eros*, in particular, needs to be purified of its sinful tendencies, otherwise it deteriorates into puerile eroticism. "Reaching out for" easily becomes "seeking to grasp for my own satisfaction." We must learn how, for the saints, "following one's heart's desire" becomes "connatural" with doing God's will in our lives.

Joy, as we have said, is what always characterizes a truly great saint. Theirs is a joy that results from head and heart being fully integrated. In this synergy, the heart leads the way, and the head sanctions the heart's discernment. The will then implements and executes what the heart and head are saying. In such an integrated, complementary subjectivity, we glimpse within ourselves the ecstasy of the Trinity, whose *perichoretic* 'unity-in-difference' our consciousness was created to reflect.

---

[95] I am indebted for this analysis to James and Myfanwy Moran, "The Battle for Person in the Heart," *The Inner Journey: Views from the Christian Tradition* (Sandpoint, ID: Morning Light Press, 2006) 101-113.

# SAINTLY HEARTS

*P*erhaps enough has been said to suggest that love (*eros*) is always something more than the will (*thymos*) stoically executing the heteronomous commands of an impersonal intellect (*nous*). Loving, willing, and knowing within the human person are meant to enjoy a *perichoretic* unity reflective of the Trinity. Within the Trinity there is always mutual submission and illumination. No one Trinitarian Person 'holds anything over' the others. The Son is 'obedient' to the Father; and the Father loves the Son. Both Son and Spirit 'proceed' from the Father. Jesus sends the Spirit. The Spirit 'drives' Jesus into the desert. Within the life of the Trinity, there is a never-ending exchange of 'commissions' and 'submissions.'

Our understanding of human loving, willing, and knowing, must be shaped and determined by this *perichoretic* interchange of love among the Persons of the Trinity. Just as the devotion of Jesus to His Father can never be reduced to an impersonal obedience to heteronomous commands, neither can love, as we understand it, simply be defined as "the will obeying the dictates of reason." Understood in the light of the Trinity, neither loving, willing, nor knowing can 'reign' over the other within the human person, any more than Father, Son, or Spirit ever 'reign' over each other. It is never a matter of opposition or submission among *eros, thymos,* and *nous* within the human person. It is always a matter of mutual illumination and reinforcement, identical though analogical to what we believe takes place within the Trinity itself.

Saints are never divided in their loving, willing, and knowing. To "know" God, for them, is to "love" Him. Theirs is a perfect integration of affectivity and reason, an organic harmony of caring and choosing. Each of their actions reflects a beautiful coordination of sensing, discerning, sanctioning, and affirming. They know how to receive without taking, how to intend without imposing. They follow their heart's desire infallibly into the heart of God.

How do they do this, we might ask? What allows saints to handle instinctively what the rest of us struggle to know and will deliberately? Clearly there is a conversion called for in order to become truly holy. To acquire a saintly heart I must break from what I know to be sin and turn full-faced towards a new and different way of living. Both intellectual and affective conversions are required. I must learn how to listen to, recognize, and discern the movements within both my heart and my head. I must learn how to attend to the varied inclinations and dispositions of my subjectivity. I must learn to know and love myself, in light of divine Revelation. This must be done in an intentional, rational, and responsible way, but also in a way that is not *merely* intentional, or *simply* rational. Love informed by Revelation is always more than the willful execution of divine commands dictated by dispassionate reason. It is rational, to be sure, but it is also supra-rational, trans-rational. Its object is God. The heart caught up in the love of Christ has reasons that the intellect knows not of. The depths of love in a person united to Jesus always exceed the capacity of the human mind to fully comprehend.

Often the noise of the mind can keep us from hearing the whisperings of the heart. Trying mechanically to negotiate moral decisions as a surrogate for passionate love of Christ never produces a saint. It is the loving disciple, not the neutral scholar, who is enabled to see Jesus in the depths of His Mystery as God. Love comes first. Love comes last. "God is love, and he who abides in love abides in God" (1 Jn. 4:16). Love is the alpha and omega, the beginning and the end, of all genuine "knowledge." To "know" Christ is to love Christ.

The heart is the honing mechanism of the human person. It intends value. It intends God. Often it gets sidetracked and inordinately attached to things of lesser value. The good is always the enemy of the best. Sin may be defined as addictive attachment to values unworthy of, and destructive of, the human person. Sin is disordered and wrongly attached love. But love is infinite and always intends infinity. Love intends God. Saintly hearts have learned how to rightly direct their love to God and others in a way that fulfills them and gives ever greater honor and glory to God. They do all this in an unforced, non-stoical way that baffles those who have been taught that following Jesus is primarily a matter of following rules and being able to recite the proper formulas. .

"If you love me, you will keep my commandments" (Jn. 14:15). This may sound like loving Jesus means primarily keeping his commandments. But we know from the story of the rich young man – as well as the many other instances of flagrant sinners loved, forgiven, and accepted by Jesus - that simply keeping the commandments, however necessary it may be to loving God, is never sufficient to attain the intimacy with Him that He desires for us. "I have kept all of these from my youth," says the rich young man, "what more must I do?" (Mt. 19:20). "Jesus, looking at him with love said, 'If you would be perfect, do, sell all that you have, give the proceeds to the poor, then come follow Me'" (Mt. 19:21). Hearing this, the young man "went away sad, for he had many possessions (Mt. 19:22). Here we catch a glimpse of how love of God always exceeds keeping the commandments. "Her sins, which are many, must have been forgiven her, for she loved much" (Lk. 7:47). Here we see the asymmetrical relation of keeping the commandments and loving Christ completely. He is able to do in and for us what we are not able to do ourselves, but only when we have given ourselves over to Him with hearts that are holding nothing back.

Extrinsic obedience is important but it does not exhaust the loving relationship that God intends for us with Himself. It is a necessary but insufficient condition for intimate union with the Trinity. Because of our fallen condition, we must acquire through deliberate obedience what comes naturally within the Divine *Communio*. We must *do* what Jesus commanded in order to become more like *Who* Jesus is. Within the Trinity, Jesus very identity is "the Obedient One." He is perfectly surrendered to the Father. His whole "being" is oriented to the Father in grateful receptivity and obedience. What comes "naturally" for the Eternal Word must be acquired by dint of effort for us fallen creatures who bear His image. In our sinful world, cognition (*nous*, intellect) directs volition (*thymos*, will) to do what Revelation directs, in order that habits of the heart (*eros*) become formed in ways that will lead to our deification in Christ.

Interestingly, the need for intentional obedience diminishes as saintly hearts are formed. A certain "attunement" to the things of God develops that makes regression to actions, attitudes, and dispositions contrary to the love of God increasingly impossible. Saints begin to do the right thing naturally, seemingly without effort. Their minds, hearts, and wills have become so "tuned in" to the voice of God that they are almost instantly and profoundly aware of the subtlest interior movement either towards or away from a deeper union with Him. What began as a deliberate, difficult "keeping the commandments" becomes, as one's spiritual life matures, "second nature," effortless, and full of joy.

Saints are like virtuosos in any field of art or science. They hear and see aspects and dimensions of reality that are unknown to those less attuned and attentive to the things of God. Their inner eyes and ears are trained as to discern and detect subtleties and nuances unperceived by those less tutored in such matters. They acquire a "connatural" affinity with the desires of God. They have "put on the mind of Christ" (1 Cor. 2:16). The value-responsiveness of their affections has been formed so as to recognize immediately the "fittingness" of their emotional responses vis-a-vis the Will of God. Through prayer and spiritual direction, their cooperation with the process of sanctification has become finely tuned, refined, and perfected. All traces of heteronomy have disappeared. They are rendered virtually incapable of making even the first movement away from the desires of God.[96]

This is true freedom. Freedom is not the license to do anything I please anytime I desire. It is the freedom from doing or saying anything that interferes with my intimacy with God and other persons. It is only

---

[96] This is the position of St. John of the Cross (eg., *Spiritual Canticle*, Stanza 25). In this, he differs from St. Teresa of Avila, who always believed in the possibility of regression in the spiritual life. See the discussion in Thomas Dubay, S.M., *Fire Within: St. Teresa of Avila, St. John of the Cross, and the Gospel – On Prayer* (San Francisco: Ignatius Press, 1989) esp. 182-188.

when we still have unconverted hearts that we must have fear-driven recourse to concepts, judgments, and will-acts as substitutes for our hearts operating in 'connatural' union with the voice of God within. Once we have learned how to discern the Wisdom of God whispering in the heart, every philosophical and theological explanation of faith, hope, and love seem pitifully lame, providing no sure guide to knowing God's Will for one's life.

All of this is simply to say it is the *heart* of the saint that governs his or her behavior. The heart of a saint is a heart formed in value-responsiveness by the Holy Spirit, and illumined by an understanding that itself has been transfigured by the light of divine revelation. It is a heart that has undergone an apprenticeship in self-awareness and self-mastery. It is a heart that knows itself through and through, while at the same time acknowledging one's "life is hidden with God in Christ" (Col. 3:3). It is a heart able to give itself away without compromising its self-possession. It is a heart that is self-transcending in the Trinitarian sense of the term. It is a heart capable of communing with objects and persons of intrinsic value independent of itself, without eviscerating itself in the process. It a heart that discovers its fulfillment in acts of self-possessed self-surrender.

For the saintly heart, emotions are no longer experienced as a threat to 'rational obedience.' They are a purified litmus screen upon which the Holy Spirit deposits traces of His call to deeper conversion and deification. A heart on fire with consolations of the Spirit becomes the *ordinary* way in which the saint experiences his or her union with God, despite the periods of aridity and desolation that God occasionally permits to test and strengthen the love of his perfect ones.[97]

This vision of perfectly integrated *eros* (heart), *thymos* (will), and *nous* (intellect) is incomprehensible to those who see disunity within the human person as a permanent part of human nature. Resigned to perpetual heteronomy within human subjectivity, they imagine the only way to "imitate Christ" is to "obey" with the "will" the "truths" Christ

---

[97] This is the position of both St. John of the Cross (see Dubay, *Fire Within*, 190-191) and St. Ignatius of Loyola (see Gallagher, *Discernment of Spirits*, 47-56).

teaches. They seek to serve Him with a resolute "will" and a stiff upper lip. This common but misguided reduction of Christian faith to moral obligation and stoic obedience is a perversion of the patristic vision of deification. The saint is the person that Jesus chose to participate in His own divine-human personhood. We are meant to live joyfully "in Christ," not simply "in dour obedience" to Him. Through the mystery of His Incarnation, His life has become our own: His ways, our ways; His mind, our mind; His heart, our heart. Once incorporated into Him through our Baptism and on-going conversion, all our thoughts, words, and deeds become supernatural. As St. John of the Cross says, "In this new life that the soul lives when it has arrived at the perfect union with God...all the inclinations and activity of the appetites and faculties...become divine."[98]

The restoration of *eros* (love, heart, affectivity) to its rightful place as the centerpiece within the triune consciousness of the human person is both a condition and a consequence of transforming union with Christ. Only by turning to this deepest of Christian mysteries – *theosis* or deification (divinization) – can we begin to comprehend what sainthood truly means. Holiness is not simply the acquisition of grace and salvation through obedience to Christ. It is the far more personal, more mystical, more contemplative incorporation of the entire human person into the divine Person of Jesus. When this occurs, our very flesh will begin to resonate with the deifying beauty and glory of the risen Lord.

---

[98] *The Living Flame of Love*, 2, n. 32.

# PART THREE

## Deified Personhood

*Section One*

# Theosis: The Goal of Deification

# INCORPORATION

$\mathcal{L}$iving "in Christ" (*en Christo*) is so much greater than "imitating Christ" as to be a fundamentally different way of imagining our vocation as Christians. What is at stake here is the equivalent of a Copernican revolution in our understanding and appreciation of the Incarnation. "God became man," says St. Athanasius, "so that man can become God."[99] What could Athanasius mean by "becoming God"? How is it possible for a human creature – a human being, a human person – to "become God?" Seeking to understand and attain to what St. Athanasius meant by "becoming God" (deification) is, for the Christian, the be all and end all of the Christian life.

This is an astounding claim. The concept of "becoming God" "in Christ" is foreign to contemporary Christians for many reasons. First of all, most of us have lost touch with, or never encountered, the patristic sources of the Christian faith from which the doctrine of deification comes. Yet, this doctrine of *theosis* – deification or divinization, "participation in the divine nature" (2 Pt. 1:4) – was the heart and soul of the theology of the early church fathers.[100] Sadly, this mystical doctrine is largely unknown to modern-day believers. For many, the Christian faith has been reduced either to a simple moralism (works righteousness) or a flimsy fideism (eternal security). Neither of these distortions of the Christian mystery satisfies the spiritual hunger that drives us towards the person of Jesus.

Secondly, and more importantly, as a result of sin in our lives – the

---

[99] *On the Incarnation*, 54, 3 (PG 25, 192B), quoted in *The Catechism of the Catholic Church* #460.

[100] The definitive work on deification is by Norman Russell, *The Doctrine of Deification in the Greek Patristic Tradition* (Oxford: Oxford University Press, 2004).

effects of Original Sin and the after-effects of our actual sins – our vision of Christ is clouded. We see "through a glass darkly" (1 Cor. 13:12), as St. Paul says. We set Jesus and ourselves side-by-side, imagining that we are somehow on the same level as Him. We see him as a creature exactly like ourselves. And while it is true that He "is like us in everything but sin" (Heb. 4:15), it is also true that He is "true God from true God, begotten, not made, one in being (*homoousion*) with the Father." He is, in other words, a divine Person, as well as a human being. He is the God-man. *He is not a human person.* He is "God become man," not "man become God." This distinction is crucial. Jesus has the power, as a divine Person, to make human beings like Himself; to elevate them, to perfect them, to fulfill them. By becoming man, He did not collapse from being God in order to become man; he became man, "assuming human nature," in order to incorporate human persons into Himself.

Trying to get our minds around this central mystery of our Christian faith is critically important. Yet, it is rendered ever more difficult because of our fallen understanding and because of our ignorance of the patristic tradition. To modern ears, the doctrine of deification sounds foreign and unpalatable. Once our perceptions are transformed by grace, however, the mystery of divinization becomes the "pearl of great price" (Mt. 13:46). It enriches our Christian faith beyond anything the utilitarian or moralistic versions of contemporary religion can offer. It unites us with the saints of every era who have known, to the very core of their being, that living "in Christ" is the real meaning of salvation.

Salvation: this is a term that reveals what is at stake in unpacking the patristic doctrine of divinization. Salvation is usually interpreted as "going to heaven" (Catholic), or "accepting Jesus as Lord and Savior" (Evangelical). Neither of these pious platitudes gets to the heart of the ancient Christian understanding of the Mystery of the Incarnation. For the early Church Fathers, Jesus did not simply appear on the earthly scene so that individuals could negotiate a right relationship with God. Still less was Jesus' mission to deliver a message or teach as a philosopher. For them, Jesus is never a means to an end. He is, on the contrary, the End itself. He is the Alpha and the Omega, the

Beginning and the End (Rev., 1:8; 21:6; 22:13). Salvation *is* Jesus Christ. He incorporates us into His Corporate (Mystical) Body, imparting to us immortality, thereby giving us a share in His Trinitarian Life. To understand salvation merely as a matter of "going somewhere" or "getting something from God" trivializes the mysterious and mystical intimacy that Christ promises to those who place their trust in Him. Christianity becomes a utilitarian and domesticated exercise in human projections when we try to reduce the redemption Christ constitutes in the Word-become-flesh to a commodity, or seek to make a claim upon it as a secured achievement.

Deification conveys the mystery of salvation to us in a way that is more dynamic, personal (existential), and eschatological than all other pedestrian, forensic (legalistic), or pragmatic models of redemption and sanctification. Deification connotes a *participation in* the Paschal Mystery of Christ. This "sharing in" the very Person and mission of Jesus Christ includes "taking part in" His Ascension and reign in glory at the right hand of the Father. In short, a living sense of *participating in the very divine Person of Jesus* is missing from the more static versions of 'working out our salvation in fear and trembling' (2 Cor. 7:15) that occupy the current ecclesiological landscape.

The doctrine of deification enjoins an upward or assumptive (assimilative) metaphor for the way in which the Spirit of Jesus incorporates the chosen of Jesus (cf. Eph. 1:3) into His Mystical Body. We are "taken up into Christ" through deification in a manner that is not adequately communicated by narratives of salvation that picture us and Jesus in a didactic or imitative relationship. Contemplation of Jesus Resurrection and Ascension is central to our appreciation of the mystery of our *theosis* in Christ.

The miracle of deification is also a greater mystery, even, than "growing in holiness." This is because *incorporation into* Jesus is infinitely deeper than merely *imitating* Christ. Deification involves the transfiguration of the whole person through an entrance into Christ's own Transfiguration and glorification. Divinization means becoming a "partaker of his divine nature" (2 Pt. 1:4). We do this by entering into, literally, the Death, Resurrection, and glorious Ascension of Jesus

Christ as Lord. Together with Christ "we are raised up and seated" at the right hand of the Father (Eph. 1:20; 2:6, 18). These are no mere figures of speech. They are not biblical hyperbole. They describe a *mystical realism* as objective as Jesus' mission itself. They are the scriptural and patristic descriptions of the Mystery of the Incarnation.

Paradigms of salvation that are not sufficiently eschatological, therefore, cannot comprehend how it is possible to enter in a mystically real way into the Paschal Mystery of Christ. They conceive of salvation as something two-dimensional, flat, and sequential. On this view, the events of Jesus death, resurrection, ascension, sending of the Holy Spirit, establishment of the Church, and Christ coming again in glory, are imagined as a series of historical happenings whose meaning is exhausted chronologically. It is forgotten that the main Actor in these historical events is the God-man Himself whose every action is theandric [both divine and human] and thus eternal. A key quote from *The Catechism of the Catholic Church* succinctly summarizes all that is at stake for the way in which we imagine the Sacrifice of Christ:

"His Paschal Mystery is a real event that occurred in our history, but it is unique: all other historical events happen once, and then they pass away, swallowed up in the past. The Paschal mystery of Christ, by contrast, cannot remain only in the past, because by his death he conquered death, and all that Christ is – all that he did and suffered for all men – participates in the divine eternity, and so transcends all times while being made present in them all. The event of the Cross and the Resurrection abides and draws everything towards life."[101]

The mysteries of the life of Christ introduce into history the *Telos* (goal, *Omega*) towards which God is drawing all things through the power of His Holy Spirit. The end of the story is introduced into the middle of the story to bathe the characters in the story with the glory of the Savior. The Eternal Word, pre-existing time, enters time by assuming flesh at a specific moment in time in order to sanctify time. He does this by incorporating all of time into the timelessness of Himself. It's as if the *meaning* of the story enters the story as a character

---

[101] *The Catechism of the Catholic Church* # 1084; cf. #1165, (emphasis added).

in the story to give the players in the story a share in the meaning of the story before the final meaning of the story is fully disclosed.[102]

Roundabout images like these are necessary to convey the highly eschatological character of the mystery of deification. The *future fulfillment* of history and creation is present in every action and in every cell of the Person of Jesus. Entrance into this Person is possible for every human person who encounters Jesus through the mysterious ways He has established.[103]

Because Jesus is a divine Person, the events of His life are not swallowed up in the past. It is more accurate to say that the events of every generation's present are kept *alive by His future*, which has been established permanently on earth in and through the events of Jesus' past. The Paschal Mystery of Jesus Passion, Death, and Resurrection include His Ascension and His coming again in glory. The *Parousia* of the Son of Man is included in His *kenosis*, suffering, and death. How can this be? It is because Christ is one Person, and His divine Person includes all the mysteries of all His comings and goings. His future glory, therefore, is also established as reality that abides with us forever, just as does His Cross and Resurrection, since it is inseparable from His Person as the Eternal Word. His coming again in glory is, and always was, of a piece with His Paschal Mystery as an historical event. Together with the Cross and Resurrection of Christ, His *future coming* even now *abides* with us and draws everything towards life in itself.

Expressing and maintaining a sense of this "multiform contemporaneity" of Christ is exceedingly difficult to do. The entropy of our darkened intellect tends to recall past events of the mystery of redemption as bygone events. This is unfortunate. It denudes the greatest mysteries of our redemption and salvation of their mystical depths and transformative power. Whenever we reduce these events

---

[102] This is the Theo-dramatic approach to the Incarnation explored so imaginatively by von Balthasar. See especially his *Theo-Drama: Theological Dramatic Theory, Volume I:* (hereafter TD, I) *Prologomena,* trans. Graham Harrison (San Francisco: Ignatius Press, 1988) 264-324.

[103] The sacramental "mysteries" create, and incorporate us into, His Mystical Body, the *Ekklesia* (Church).

into something we call "the life *of* Christ," we are hindered from seeing that life "*in* Christ" is an existential possibility for us in Jesus' future-made-present.

The Kingdom of God was at the center of Jesus preaching. "Behold, the kingdom of God is at hand...the kingdom of God is in your midst." (Lk. 17:21). This is also the early Christian *kerygma*. It is the core of the gospel proclamation. What does it mean? How are we to understand the urgency with which Jesus and the early Church announced the advent of the Kingdom? One possible translation might be: "There is a new Lord of this world; there is a new King of all creation!" Both Jesus and the early Church had an immediate sense of the apocalyptic "breaking in" of the Father's Reign over all of creation through the Incarnation of His Son. The Powers and Principalities holding the world in bondage since the sin of Adam and Eve have been defeated (Eph. 3:10; 6:12). Their stranglehold on the cosmos from the beginning of time has been broken. Jesus has "made a public display of them, triumphing over them" in His life, death, and resurrection (Col. 2:15).

This electrifying sense of the King of King's incarnate Presence is neutralized and brought to ground by a pedestrian theology and spirituality that separates Christ's heavenly glory from our earthly existence. Our vision of deification is greatly dimmed if we view the return of Christ in glory as a future, faraway reality, anticipated at best in the one-to-one personal judgment after death. This is a terrible evisceration of the power of Paschal Mystery. When the *kairos* of Jesus' coming is turned into a series of mere *chrono*logical events, the divinizing mystery of the Word-made-flesh is reduced to a moralistic message and loses the power to save those yearning for a Savior.

Jesus is "the Incarnate One who is, who was, and who is to come" (Rev. 1:4, 8; 11:17). In Him, all time has been fulfilled. He is, *in His very Person,* the Kingdom of God. He replaces and fulfills all pre-figurements of God's salvation. He is the New Torah and the New Temple. We search in vain for a historical unfolding or a future event that supersedes Jesus. In giving us His Son, the Father has spoken His definitive Word. There is nothing to add to revelation. His entrance into time 2,000 years ago introduced the *fullness* of time (*kairos*) into chronological time (*chronos*). He is now present in history, forever gathering all things unto Himself.

To "remember" Jesus is always to be doing something more than simply "calling Him to mind" or having a mental recollection of His deeds or actions. Our *anamnesis* (recalling) of Jesus is, quite literally and mystically, a re-constituting of His Presence through the interior assent of faith. Through the power of the Holy Spirit, it is now possible to enter into the very Person of Christ Himself. He is a Corporate Person with a Mystical Body. The presence of His future glory, revealed, concealed, and abiding in our midst, makes possible the deification and "christification" of those who enter into to the "memorial" of His Paschal Mystery.

His Paschal Mystery, including His Ascension and 2$^{nd}$ Coming, is established firmly in the center of history. Like a divine magnet, this Mystery draws all who are predestined to enter His eternal glory into that same glory-made-present (Eph. 1:4-5). His Paschal Mystery elevates and perfects, enfolds and fulfills, incorporates and instantiates, assimilates and differentiates, all those "chosen before the foundation of the world" to be adorers of the Lamb who was slain (Rev.5:6, 9, 12; 13:8). We are members of Christ's *Totus Corpus Mysticum*. Deification is what occurs when those "he has called to Himself" are, even now (Jn. 4:23; 5:25), taken into his future glory through assimilation into His Paschal Mystery. The once-only events of the chronological past - Christ's death, resurrection, and ascension - abide now forever as His future-made-present. Entering into this eschatological Mystery, we become "partakers of the divine nature" (2 Pt. 1:4), divinized "indwellers" of the Most Holy Trinity (Jn. 17:3, 21-24). Once *incorporated* into the Person of Jesus Christ, we are enabled to imitate Him as a natural by-product of our assimilation into Him.

# THEOSIS

*heosis* is the most accurate term describing the patristic doctrine of deification or divinization. To become a "partaker of the divine nature" (2 Pt. 1:4) is to become deified or divinized. It is to experience the mystery of "christification." It is to become a living theophany of the love of God. It is to "participate" in the very life of the Trinity through incorporation into the Person of Jesus Christ.

It is now time to explore in greater detail the early church consensus that "God became man so that man could become God." The Fathers are unanimous in this assertion. This mystery is also sometimes called the "divine exchange." As St. Ephraim the Syrian said, "We gave him humanity, He gave us divinity."[104] This "admirable exchange" (*admirable commercium* or *tantum quantum*) indicates the mysterious and paradoxical way in which the *kenosis* (self-emptying) of the Word-made-flesh becomes the *theosis* of those who become "partakers of the divine nature" (2 Pt. 1:4). Jesus' *kenosis* is our *theosis*. To live "in Christ," means to become deified. To be united hypostatically to Jesus is to become divinized through our "incorporation" or "assimilation" into Him. *Theosis* is the purpose of the Incarnation, and the signature doctrine of patristic Christianity.

*Theosis* (deification, divinization) is to be immediately and radically differentiated from the heretical views of man's *absorption* into God (monism). Pantheism, eternal progression, quietism, and other heterodox beliefs that picture human persons as somehow melding into the Divine Essence are perversions of the patristic doctrine of *theosis*. We are "*partakers* in the divine nature" (2 Pt. 1:4); we are not usurpers

---

[104] Quoted in Russell, *The Doctrine of Deification in the Greek Patristic Tradition*, 322.

of it. *Theosis* is not the belief that we are God in His Essence. It is not the belief that we change into God or that God replaces a part or all of us. According to the doctrine of deification, God remains God by nature, and man remains man by nature. At the same time, in *theosis*, the human person comes to "participate" in the very Triune Life of God. We become "by participation" what God is "by nature." To quote St. Augustine: "He became a *partaker* in our weakness, bestowing on us a *participation* in his divinity" (*Commentary on Ps. 58*).

*Theosis* is the anthropological corollary of the Trinitarian Mystery. As St. Maximus the Confessor puts it, man becomes God "in the same degree as he who is God by nature partook of our weakness when he became incarnate."[105] Here we see the difference between Christian *communio* and the heresies of pantheistic or monistic union. The goal of *theosis* is communion with God in which the human person "partakes of" the divine nature without thereby becoming divine by nature. The goal of *theosis*, in other words, is *relationship*, not identity.[106] The identity neither of God nor of man is threatened in *theosis*. Instead, God share His divinity with man in such a way that the *image* of God in which he was created blossoms into full *likeness*.

As mentioned before, many, if not most, Christians have never heard of *theosis*, despite the fact that it is taproot teaching of ancient Church teaching. Scripture, Tradition, and *The Catechism of the Catholic Church* shine resplendently with the glory of this unfathomable mystery; yet, the concept of deification remains as foreign to many modern day Christians as do the eastern churches where this doctrine originally flourished. This is not surprising. Even the original proponents of *theosis* found it difficult to articulate fully the breadth and depth of this transcendental truth. This mystery, says St. Macarius of Egypt (c. 300-390), is so "subtle and profound" that "though we dare to write about deification...to describe it [adequately] is beyond our skill" (*Philokalia* 3:314). St. Gregory Palamas, one of the greatest proponents

---

[105] Russell, *The Doctrine of Deification in the Greek Patristic Tradition*, 283.

[106] See the same distinction made by Cardinal Joseph Ratzinger, *Behold the Pierced One* (San Francisco: Ignatius Press, 1986) 86.

of divinization, was of the same opinion (*Defense of the Holy Hesychasts* 3.1.32). St. Maximus the Confessor sums up the Tradition about *theosis* when he says: "All that God is, *except for an identity in ousia* (nature, essence), man becomes when he is deified by grace" (*Philokalia*, 2:193).

*Theosis* is the realization of the Trinity's eternal desire to re-establish a connubial union with a fallen world. *Theosis* is the grace of the Holy Spirit, made possible by the Paschal Sacrifice of the Son, which mysteriously "assimilates" the human person into the *Communio Personarum* of the Trinity. Our deification in Christ parallels and participates in the hypostatic union that exists within the Trinitarian Life itself. It occurs "without confusion or change" of both human nature and the Divine Nature. In divinization, the human person is conformed perfectly to the divine image and likeness of God, permeated and suffused with the Life and Love of the Trinity. As Pope Benedict XVI has said, commenting upon the *admirable commercium,* which he describes as the heart of the gospel: "This exchange consists of God taking our human existence on himself in *order to bestow his divine existence on us,* of his choosing our nothingness in order to give his plenitude."[107] It is difficult, even in the patristic literature, to find a better description of the doctrine of deification.

It bears repeating, lest misunderstanding creep in, that *theosis* involves no lessening or alteration of either the human or the divine natures. It is a *non-competitive coinherence* of God with man, and man with God. Deification of the human person is an extension of the doctrine of the *hypostatic* union of the inseparable but unconfused union of the divine and human natures in Christ. In *theosis,* we are speaking of the *hypostatic* union of the divine Person of Jesus with the individual human persons who are assimilated into Him through faith, the sacraments, and the power of the Holy Spirit. The assumption of the human person into Christ, and hence into the very life of the Trinitarian *Communio,* constitutes the divine indwelling that Jesus speaks so mystically about

---

[107] Pope Benedict XVI, *Dogma and Preaching,* trans. Matthew J. O'Connell (Chicago, IL: Franciscan Herald Press, 1985) 84, cited in Daniel Keating, *Deification and Grace* (Naples, FL: Sapientia Press, 2007) 16 (emphasis added).

in His high priestly prayer: "That we may be one, Father, just as you are in me and I in you, that they are in us and You are in them" (John 17:11, 22-23, 26). *Theosis* unites the human person to the Father in Christ through the power of the Holy Spirit. The Spirit imparts to such a person "all that is God except His essence as God." This includes all the attributes, gifts, and powers of God. One becomes not only a son, but also an heir (Gal. 4:7). This adoptive kinship includes all the entitlements that accompany incorporation into the Sonship of Christ. One is "begotten" of God because he is incorporated into the "only begotten" Son of God.

The following is a sampling of patristic texts testifying to the power of *theosis* and the *tantum-quantum* (divine exchange) in the early Christian Tradition:

- *The Son of God became what we are in order to make us what he is in himself (St. Irenaeus, 130-200 a.d.)*
- *He became human that we might become divine (St. Athanasius, 295-373 a.d.)*
- *The heavenly Spirit touched humanity [in Jesus] and brought it to divinity (Pseudo-Macarius, 300-390 a.d.)*
- *He gave us divinity, we gave him humanity (St. Ephrem the Syrian, 306-373 a.d.)*
- *Divinity flew down to draw humanity up (St. Ephrem the Syrian)*
- *...we become God to the same extent that He became man" (St. Gregory Nazianzen, 329-389)*
- *Let us become gods for His sake, since He became man for our sake (St. Gregory Nazianzen)*
- *The Logos became Son of Man, while being true Son of God, in order to make children of God out of the children of human beings (St. John Chrysostom, 347-407)*
- *The Son of God became the Son of Man that he might make the sons of men the sons of God (St. Augustine, 354-430)*
- *He became a partaker in our weakness, bestowing on us a participation in his divinity (St. Augustine)*

- *He accepts what belongs to us, taking it to himself as his own, and…gives us in exchange what belongs to him (St. Cyril of Alexandria, d. 444)*
- *Man's ability to deify himself through love for God's sake is correlative to God's becoming man through compassion for man's sake (St. Maximus the Confessor, 560-622)*
- *The mystery…is the emptying out of the divine nature, the union of God and man, and the deification of the manhood that was assumed (St. Andrew of Crete, 660-740*
- *God received his human flesh from the Virgin Mary and gave her divinity instead; now he gives his flesh to his saints to deify them (St. Symeon the New Theologian, 949-1022)*
- *The Only-begotten Son of God, wanting us to be partakers of his divinity, assumed our human nature so that, having become man, he might make men gods (St. Thomas Aquinas, 1225-1274)*
- *Why should we not become 'gods' for Him who for love of us became man (St. Bernard of Clairvaux, 1153)*

One could go on at length quoting Church Fathers and Doctors of the Church, both East and West, who promote the doctrine of divinization.[108] These progenitors of our faith saw themselves as drawing out the hidden meaning of the Incarnation. They consider humanity's "organic union" with the Triune God to be the central theme in the letters of St. Paul and the gospel of St. John. The Tradition views the doctrine of *theosis* as the full flowering of the mission of Christ and the mystical vision of St. Paul and the Apostles.

Biblical texts abound testifying to the centrality of deification in the mission and message of Christ. Many of these texts were read by the Fathers as a commentary upon, and the culmination of, the promise made by the Psalms that "Ye shall be as gods" (Ps. 82:6). The key New Testament text regarding *theosis* is 2 Pt. 1:4: He made

---

[108] In addition to the works of Russell and Keating cited above, see Olivier Clement, *The Roots of Christian Mysticism: Texts from the Patristic Era with Commentary* for citation about *theosis* from the Christian East, and V. Rev. Dr. Michael Azkoul, *Ye Are Gods: Salvation According to the Latin Fathers* (Dewdney, Canada: Synaxis Press, 2002) for a collection of texts on deification from the Western (Latin) Fathers.

us..."partakers of the divine nature." The letters of Paul (especially Ephesians and Colossians), as well as the gospel of John (3:8; 14:21-23; 15:4-8; 17:21-23; 1 John 3:2; 4:12), are particularly rich in their witnesses to the centrality of the doctrine of divinization. 2 Corinthians 8:9, for example, provides a good example of the *admirabile commercium*: "... for your sake he [Jesus] became poor, though being rich, so that by his poverty, you may become rich." The Fathers read this exchange formula in light of Philippians 2:5-11, where Jesus "empties himself... was born...and became obedient unto death...thus God highly exalted Him..." His *kenosis* is our *theosis*. By entering into the Paschal Mystery of Christ, we enter into the glory of the One who "emptied Himself" for our sake on the Cross.

St. Paul, as we have seen, uses the phrase "in Christ" (*en Christo*) over 164 times in his epistles. Many scholars have drawn attention to the fact that at the heart of Paul's mystical theology is the formula "in Christ" or its equivalent expression "in Christ Jesus" or "in the Lord."[109] It is important to note that many, if not most, of these references are *ontological*, not merely psychological statements. They denote a *mystical relationship* between the human person and Christ, such that *the very being* of the person is transfigured when encountering the Divine Person of Jesus. In this St. Paul is both recalling his own transformative encounter with Jesus on his way to Damascus (Acts 9:1-19), as well as drawing out the mystical implications of what it means to know Jesus in His resurrected existence. It is important to note that when Saul first heard the voice of Jesus, "Saul, Saul, why are you persecuting Me?" (Acts 9:4), he was encountering Christ as a *Corporate* Person, intimately and ontologically united with the members of His Mystical Body. Here Jesus identifies Himself with the very *communio personarum* whom Saul is persecuting. Converted in light of this mystical identification, St. Paul spends the rest of his life working out the implications of living and being "in Christ."

---

[109] See the brilliant recapitulation of Pauline mysticism, particular regarding St. Paul's "doctrine of participation," in James D. G. Dunn, *The Theology of Paul the Apostle* (Grand Rapids, MI: William B. Eerdmans Publishing Co., 2006) 390-410.

These New Testament texts concerning *theosis* were prepared for and foreshadowed by key Old Testament texts (e.g., Ex. 22:28, Ps. 82:1-7) where the Judges of Israel are called "gods," and where Moses, in particular, having encountered God in the theophany of the burning bush, became *"like God* to Pharaoh" (Ex. 7:1). Moses also encountered God "as one who spoke to Him face to face" (Ex. 33:11). As a result of such encounters, Moses was so transfigured that his countenance shone with the glory of the Lord (Ex. 34:30). The radiant face of Moses, incandescent with the uncreated light of God, becomes a harbinger of his appearance with Jesus at the Transfiguration in the New Testament (Mt. 17:1-8). Moses' countenance and conversion is an enduring image of *theosis* in the lives of those who "participate" in Christ. It is no coincidence that Moses is present together with Elijah speaking with Jesus during His Transfiguration on Mt. Tabor (Mk. 9:2ff.).

Daniel Keating has summarized the biblical foundation for the doctrine of deification by making the following points:

- The exchange formula ("the Son of God became the Son of Man, so that the sons of men might become the sons of God") is anchored in the exchange Paul speaks of in 2 Corinthians 8:9.
- The centerpiece of divine filiation – becoming "sons of God" – is found in both Paul and John (Gal. 4:4-6; Rom. 8:14-17, 29; 1 Jn. 3:1-2)
- The notion of becoming "gods" is rooted in a Christological interpretation of Psalm 82:6 (Jn. 10:34-35), and our vocation to be "partakers of the divine nature" is directly stated in 2 Peter 1:4.
- The goal of our redemption as transformation into his image and likeness is described by Paul (Rom. 8:29; 2 Cor. 3:18); the New Testament teaching on maturity (Mt. 5:48; Heb. 5:14; 6:1; 1 Cor. 14:20; Col. 1:28; Eph. 4:13; Jas. 1:4) and growth in virtue (2 Pt. 1:5-8; Rom. 13:12-14; Gal. 5:19-24; Eph. 4:17-32; Col. 3:5-17) show what results from a person deified in Christ

- Deification as including an ongoing participation in the death, resurrection, and ascension of Christ is attested by Paul (2 Coor 4:10-12; Phil. 3:7-11; Rom. 8:17).
- The use of the concept of "participation" by the Fathers is grounded in and confirmed by the biblical description of our redemption in Christ in terms of participation and sharing (Heb. 2:14; 2 Pt. 1:4; Heb. 6:4; 2 Cor. 13:13; Phil. 2:1; 1 Cor. 10:14-22).
- The overarching biblical narrative for the doctrine of deification is Christ as the New Adam (1 Cor. 15:22), a theme that St. Irenaeus used to buttress his use of Christus Tri-forme, linking in divine continuity Creation and Redemption, Nature and Grace, Old Covenant and New Covenant, Christ and His Church, and the Eucharist and the Wedding Feast of the Lamb.
- The doctrine of divinization is a biblically and doctrinally rich elaboration of what Paul states as our destiny in 1 Corinthians 15:47: "Just as we have borne the image of the man of dust, we shall also bear the image of the man of heaven." [110]

---

[110] Daniel Keating, *Deification and Grace*, 117-118.

# PARTICIPATION

$\mathcal{T}$here are many synonyms for the mystery of *theosis* used by the Fathers. It is variously called: transformation, union, participation, partaking, intermingling, elevation, incorporation, interpenetration, transmutation, commingling, assimilation, assumption, reintegration, adoption, transfiguration, or re-creation. Each of these descriptions brings to light a different dimension of the mystery. Deification involves being *penetrated and permeated* with the Life of God. Incorporated into the Eternal Word, human nature is raised above itself without thereby ceasing to be itself. Divinization is the epitome of "transcendent selfhood." The human person is made more fully human by being taken, whole and entire, into the Triune *Communio Personarum*. Deification establishes and secures the integrity of true human "being."

St. John of the Cross describes this same mystical mystery when he compares the divinization of the soul to the perfectly clear window penetrated with the unobstructed light, or to a log of wood made incandescent by the fire such that it is consumed yet not destroyed (cf. Ex. 3:2).[111] The window and the log "participate" in the light and fire that interpenetrate them, yet they are neither destroyed nor diminished by being "permeated" by these "higher powers." They are like the Burning Bush that was enveloped by fire "but not consumed" (Ex. 3:2). These are stellar examples of how the Higher Power penetrates the lesser without being diminished or changed by it, and how the lesser being "shares in," "participates in," and is transformed by the Higher Power without becoming identical with it. The lower being

---

[111] E.g., *The Ascent of Mount Carmel*, II, 5, 6; *The Living Flame of Love*, I, 4, 19-24.

"participates" in the Higher Power, but the Higher Power itself is "unparticipatable." The lesser beings are inundated but not destroyed by the deifying Higher Power. The window and the log become "purified" and "perfected" by being "taken up into" the energy of the light and fire that make them incandescent.

Deification, then, implies an influx of Divine Life causing human life to come to perfection by "participating in" but not "changing into" the nature of Him Who penetrates it with His Love. There is an "intertwining" of the person with Christ, without compromise either of the Divine or human *[H]ypostasis*. Deification is never a melding, blending, or absorption of the person with Christ. It does not result in a loss of personal identity. Rather, one discovers one's true identity when one has been fully incorporated into Christ.

Nuptial union is yet another metaphor, model, image, and analogy, for the deifying interpenetration of God's life in *theosis*. Maximus the Confessor calls *theosis* an "erotic union" (*Philokalia* 2:216). St. Macarius the Great and St. John Chrysostom also use the analogy of marriage to define the intimacy and dynamic of what takes place when God becomes man in order to deify man. Just as man and woman, in their one-flesh union, maintain the integrity of their separate identities, yet form a single existence and hold all things in common, so the Christian is joined to God in an "ineffable communion" (cf. 1 Cor. 6:15-17) in the mystery of divinization.

Pope John Paul II's *Theology of the Body* is inspired by this same deifying vision of the nuptial Mystery. He sees the one-flesh union of man and woman in marriage as the sacramental icon of divinization. Marriage is a symbolic instantiation of the Hypostatic Union the Holy Spirit effects between Christ and His Bride, the Church. We can extend this nuptial image to include the Incarnation and the Trinitarian *Communio Personarum*. The one-flesh union of man and woman in marriage is an echo of, as well as a participation in, the more primordial nuptial *ek-stasis* that exists among Father, Son, and Holy Spirit. "If the goal of God's dealings with the world is *connubium*, then this union is realized when by Baptism the believer is inserted into Christ's body. From that moment Christ impresses his form upon the Christian. From that moment the life of the Christian consists in daily letting himself be molded by the archetypal figure of Christ."[112]

It is the patristic concept of "participation" (*methexis, koinonia*) that best describes the mystery of our deification in Christ. What does it mean to say we "participate" in the life of the Trinity? What does it mean to say we are "assimilated" into Jesus? What is the meaning of calling us "partakers" of the divine nature (2 Pt. 1:4)? The concept of "participation" (*methexis*) is the preferred means by which the Fathers sought to convey the hypostatic coinherence between the human person and the Trinity in and through the Incarnation.

In the patristic tradition, "participation" means something quite different from our modern understanding of this term. It doesn't mean, as we might think, to "be actively involved in" something. The emphasis is less active, more passive. To "participate" in the divine nature is more a matter of what one receives from God than what one may be trying to initiate by one's own efforts. The concept of "participation" in the Fathers derives from the philosophical tradition of Plato. It was then re-shaped by the saints to convey how redemption in Christ restored (recapitulated) all of creation to a state of fulfillment and immortality that was better, even, than our first parents enjoyed with God before the Fall.

In Platonic philosophy, "participation" describes how concrete specimens of a larger "kind" (form) "partake" of the "essence" ("nature") of this larger [and therefore, for Plato, more "real"] form (or kind). For Plato, "essences" ("natures" or "forms") precede particulars. Therefore, particular things (beings, objects, even persons) *derive their being* from pre-existing forms. "Tree-ness," for example – the "essence" or "form" of "being a tree" – pre-exists and makes possible the appearance of individual, specific trees. The "nature" of a tree exists in the mind of God before the creation of any particular trees, and endures after specific trees have come and gone. Similarly, a quality like holiness pre-exists holy persons who "participate" in the mystery

---

[112] John O'Donnell, S.J., "Hans Urs von Balthasar: The Form of His Theology," *Communio: International Catholic Review,* 16 (Fall 1989) 471.

of holiness. A holy person is an entity distinct from holiness, yet can be defined as "holy" because she or she "has a share in" holiness. Without the reality of holiness, there is no holy person; at the same time, the holy person has an existence separate from holiness. To say that the holy person "participates" in holiness, then, indicates a relationship that is at once real and analogical. It is relationship that is "substantial," i.e., not just a matter of appearance (*maya*), yet it is also asymmetrical, i.e., not a relationship between realities of equal weight (being). In this philosophical perspective, the general precedes the specific. The general is also more real (weightier, more primordial, ontologically more substantial) than the specific. Essence precedes existence. Things in existence *derive their life from* pre-existing essences (forms, natures).

This philosophical belief allowed the Fathers to do two very important things. It allowed them to account for both the similarity and differences between objects of *different ontological weight*, while accounting for a certain relation of dependence between them. In other words, "participation" occurs when an entity of one kind of being is *defined* in relation to an entity of a different kind (degree, weight) of being. A specific tree "participates in" the "nature" of trees, for example, but does not exhaust the meaning or reality of "tree-ness." A holy person "participates" in the reality of God's holiness, but does not in any way change, alter, effect, or diminish this pre-existing attribute in God. The "essence" or "nature" of super-natural qualities is neither diminished nor enhanced by the appearance of individual entities that "participate" in them. Individuals derive their being from the pre-existing power of the "natures" or "forms" of those transcendental realities in which they "have a share." Essences (natures, forms) are ontologically prior to the objects that "partake" of them. Objects "participate" in forms; forms do not participate in objects.

Applying these insights to the relationship of God to the world, and the Incarnation to the fallen human race, the Fathers were able to illustrate both the dependence of all things on the Father as Creator and the possibility for the restoration of all things to their pre-lapsarian splendor through "participation" in Christ. The world, as created, "participates" in the creative love of God. That is to say, it "derives its being" from God's initial and sustaining creative act. Created being "participates" in God, but God does not "participate" in created being. God is, as the Fathers said, "un-participatable." Similarly, when "assimilated" or "assumed" into Christ, fallen humanity "receive a share in" His divine life. Human nature comes to "partake of" or "participate in" His divine nature. "In Christ," we are capable of becoming "partakers of the divine nature" (2 Pt. 1:4). We become "by participation" what Jesus, the eternal Word, is "by nature."

The concept of "participation," therefore, guarantees both a true relation and an abiding distinction between the Source and objects of "participation." There is "room in God" for the entire world without either the world or God suffering a compromise in their respective identities. The divine life that comes from "participation" in Christ is, yes, *derivative* from His incomprehensible essence as God. But, it is none the less real, and no less a real "share" in that which makes Jesus God.

The doctrine of "participation" necessarily requires a relation between two things that are *unequal* – God and man, trees and the "nature" of trees – and these things remain unequal and distinct throughout the act of the one (the lesser) "participating" in the other (the higher). That which "participates" [i.e., fallen man] in the other, possesses the quality it receives [divinity] only in part; that which is "participated in" [i.e., God], necessarily possesses that quality fully and by nature. At the same time, the similarity between God and man, is so strongly enhanced in "participation" (*theosis*) that saints from Maximus the Confessor to John of the Cross can say that "in Christ," "the soul *becomes God from God* through participation in him and in his attributes...[and] the fullness of God permeates [the deified person] wholly as the soul permeates the body...and the whole person, as the object of divine action, is divinized by being made God by the grace of God who became man."[113]

We can see now how this patristic concept of "participation" "in God" is more personal, organic, and ontological than more prosaic

---

[113] St. John of the Cross, *Living Flame of Love*, 3, 8; Maximus the Confessor, *Ambigua 7*, cited in Keating, *Deification and Grace*, 111.

explanations of participation as "taking part in" an event. On the patristic view, "full and active participation" in the liturgy, for example, would mean something fundamentally different from "making a lot of noise" or "having a lot to say." It would be something more profound, more mystical, more transformative than "taking part" in an activity.

"Participation in Christ" means to "indwell" Jesus. It means to "take up our abode" in Him, not metaphorically but ontologically. In deification, we "participate" in Christ as organically as branches "participate" in the vine, or a baby "participates" in the womb of its mother. We "participate" in the Trinity in the sense that we "derive our being" [natural and supernatural] from Him. The Triune God is the "Source and Giver of life." Through His Incarnation, our human nature is assimilated and engrafted into His divine nature, giving us a "share" in His immortality. Persons so engrafted "into Christ" remain human persons, yet they become God "by participation."

Because "assimilation" or "assumption" into Jesus through His Incarnation is not "absorption," the concept of "participation" does not threaten the distinction between God and His creation, just as it never impedes the difference between Christ and those who "partake of His divine nature." On the contrary, it actually secures and guarantees these distinctions. As we have seen before, the immutability and impassibility of God are not compromised by the assumptive power of the Incarnation. Instead, they are its source and wellspring. Just as he *monarchia* of the Father secures the redemptive *exousia* (power, authority) of the Son, so the assimilative power of the Son in His Incarnation affirms and perfects the contingent being of the persons incorporated into Him.

When we are taken "up into Christ," we become more truly, more perfectly the human persons God created and intended us to be. "There is no human personhood that is not constituted by a union with the divine persons."[114] Not only are the effects of sin taken away, but we are also "recapitulated" (renewed and restored) in Christ in such a manner

---

[114] John Zizioulas, "Human Capacity and Human Incapacity: A Theological Exploration of Personhood," *Scottish Journal of Theology* 28 (1975) 416, cited by Douglas

that we are restored to a condition more pristine that the one enjoyed by our first parents before their Fall. "O happy fault," we proclaim at the Easter Vigil, referring to the Original Sin, "that won for us so great a Redeemer." When living "in Christ," our condition is greater and more glorious that the Original Unity in the Garden of Eden. "Participation" in God through Christ is the elevation of human life into the divine life of the Trinity. At the same time, it is the perfection of finite existence in all its beautiful, contingent, and ontological *difference* from the Lord who completes it.

A very important motto in the early Church further illumines the doctrine of participation: "That which is not assumed is not healed" ("*quod non assumpsit, non sanavit*"). "Assumption" (without absorption) into the triune life of God through Christ is the epicenter of the Christian mystery. Such is the purpose and the end of the Incarnation. "Participation" in Father, Son, and Holy Spirit is the *telos* (goal) for which we are created and redeemed. The human person is truly human only "in God." The mystery of *theosis* challenges us to go beyond seeing "God in the world" and to begin seeing "the world in God." "In Him we live, and move, and have our being," St. Paul tells us (Acts 17-28). This, in a scriptural nutshell, is the mystery of "participation." Participation in God through Christ is the perfection and completion of being human. Because God has become man, man can become God.

Astounding claims like this are commonplace in the patristic tradition because *methexis* ("participation" in God) was the taproot of their theology. "In Christ, the whole fullness of deity dwells bodily" (Col. 2:9). For those who "indwell" Jesus, the whole fullness of the Eternal Word also dwells within them. This is the miracle and synergy of divinization. This mystery cannot be too frequently or too deeply contemplated. The mind and heart must themselves be deified to begin to comprehend deification. "Participation in the Holy Spirit," says St. Cyril of Alexandria, gives human beings the grace to be shaped as

---

H. Knight, *The Theology of John Zizioulas: Personhood and the Church* (Burlington, VT: Ashgate Publishing Limited, 2007) 20.

"a complete copy of the divine nature."[115] "God himself is the life of those who participate in Him," says Irenaeus.[116] To live "in Christ" is to share "by participation" all the powers and attributes God possesses "by nature." "The deified person, while remaining completely human in nature, becomes God in both body and soul through participation in God's divine nature. The grace and the divine brightness of the beatifying glory of God permeate the whole person who gives himself over to the process of *theosis*.

"Participation" in Christ is also an anticipation and foretaste of the *Parousia*. When all is finally and fully incorporated into the Person of Jesus, the world itself will show forth the radiance of the resurrected Lord. The divinized person, partaking in the divine nature of Christ, shares in the light of Mount Tabor both before and after death. The saints are already bathed in the glory of the risen and ascended Lord. Such persons, "having become God by deification, no longer display any energy other than the divine. In everything from now on there is only one energy belonging to God."[117] For the person divinized in Christ, his or her every thought, word, and deed are those of the Trinity itself. [118]

---

[115] St. Cyril of Alexandria, *Treasure* 33 (PG 75, 228), cited in Clement, *The Roots of Christian Mysticism: Texts from the Patristic Era with Commentary*, 264.

[116] St. Irenaeus of Lyons, *Against Heresies*, V,7,1 (SC p. 153,86-88), cited in Clement, *ibid.*, 265.

[117] St. Maximus the Confessor, *Ambigua*, 7 (PG 91,1076), cited in Clement, *ibid.*, 267.

[118] See for example, St. John of the Cross, *Spiritual Canticle*, Stanza 39, Section 4.

# *Leitourgia: The Means of Deification*

# HOMO ADORANS

*D*eification (*theosis*) does not occur in a vacuum. It is neither a private nor individualistic project. It happens in communion. It happens in communion with God, and with those who have been "incorporated" into God. "Participation" in God is always "personalist participation." It is never simply a philosophical matter of "human nature" "sharing in" the "divine nature," or of the human person "participating in" the impersonal "essence" or "energies" of "God.". *Methexis* (participation) for the Christian is always essentially *koinonia* (community). God, in Christ, has a human face. To be "taken up into the Trinity" is to encounter the Persons of Jesus, His Father, and their Holy Spirit. It is no nameless, faceless "absorption" into the divine. It is an *intimate exchange* with the Persons of the Trinity through nuptial union with the Incarnate Word.

Philosophy is what takes center state when ***theo***-logy is lost. The "fatal cleavage" of theology from spirituality (prayer) and the tragic divorce of philosophy from theology reflect and reinforce the power of sin in the world. Our non-divinized intellect makes it difficult for us to appreciate the personal dimensions of the mystery of "participation" in Christ. When we are unable to clearly apprehend the miracle of *theosis*, we tend to interpret Jesus as a *symbol* of a pre-existing theological system. Or we view "participation" as an impersonal, philosophical construct. We must not underestimate how powerfully original sin has affected our theological reflection.

Before Original Sin entered the world, none of the dichotomies that currently bedevil theology and philosophy were seen to exist. There was no separation, for example, between the sacred and the secular. The secular world *was* a sacred world. The world and all it contained was experienced by Adam and Eve as a means of communion with the God, their Creator. Adam and Eve walked with Lord in the cool of the Garden (Gen. 3:8). For them, intimacy with God and with each other was natural. Everything in Paradise conveyed to them a sense of union with God. Everything was sacramental in the fullest sense of the word. Everything communicated to them the love and presence of the Trinity. The "ate with their eyes." They "drank in" everything the saw. There was no gap between what they saw, what they knew, and what they believed. To "see" was to "taste" the goodness of the Lord.

In this state of "the Original Unity,"[119] gratitude to God came to our first parents automatically. Thankfulness did not require a determined act of the will. Praise issued from them spontaneously. Their entire existence was priestly and "eucharistic." They were perpetually thankful. They experienced all they received as a total gift. And, all they beheld drew them closer into *koinonia* and intimacy with their Creator. In this primeval state of perfect communion, lust and possessiveness, as we experience them, were unknown. The hearts and minds of Adam and Eve were completely pure. They saw in each other an icon of the Trinitarian *Communio* from which they were created and into whose infinite, erotic, and *ek-static* embrace they are invited to "participate." *Eros* had none of the fallen overtones it has for us. "Intercourse" for them – both as a concept and a reality - was experienced as a sacramental "participation" in the *communio* of the Trinity. It was of a piece with their inseparable relationship (*schesis*) with God. Their nuptial intimacy with God was experienced both as the source and purpose of their union with each other.

In this state of Original Unity, our first parents also experienced the world as a banquet. It was a "feast," communicating to them "the fullness of life." The "world" did not yet "lie in wickedness" (cf. Rom. 1:29). They had not yet "fallen." They experienced directly the goodness of creation. They could, in a sense, taste the beauty "deep down in things" (Hopkins). To see the world, for them, was to "taste the goodness of the Lord." The world was "food" for their eyes. If you

---

[119] John Paul II, TB, 156ff.

had asked Adam and Eve, "Why are you here on earth?" they might have replied, like the pagan thinker, Anaxagoras, "To behold."

To "feast" their eyes on the world was also, for Adam and Eve, devoid of covetedness. Their "hunger" was for God. Their desires were ordered "above" themselves so as to allow them to experience each other and creation as gifts from God. The *eros* that burned in their hearts was perfectly and properly ordered. The gifts given to our first parents in the Garden appeared as having an autonomy and integrity of their own, yet they also served as divinely-given means of communion with God and each other. Put succinctly: Adam and Eve experienced the world "in God." They saw all things as coming from Him and leading back to Him. The world was experienced by them as a natural sacrament of communion. Everything spoke to them of God and beckoned them to God. They desired nothing "apart from God." The world existed with its own density and diversity of forms; yet, everything summoned them into a deeper communion with the One who created it.

Joy and thanksgiving characterize the lives of Adam and Eve in the Garden. They enjoyed a *priestly* life in which lustful desire and possessive craving were totally unknown. No *cult* of religious practice was either needed or considered. The world itself was experienced as a sacrament. Creation itself gave praise to God. Thanksgiving was as natural as breathing. For them, to see was to love, and to love was to praise. In their very constitution, Adam and Eve were "*homo adorans*:" persons who adore.[120] They were priests by nature. Naturally, automatically, without thought or hesitation, they offered unceasing sacrifices of praise and adoration to the God who made them. Re-kindling this pre-lapsarian vision, we can see that adoration belongs by nature to the mystery of the human person. Human existence in its

---

[120] I am indebted for the key ideas in this section to Alexander Schmemann, *For the Life of the World* (Crestwood, NY: St. Vladimir's Seminary Press, 2004). See also the books of Fr. Schmemann's student and theological heir, David Fagerberg: *Theologia Prima: What is Liturgical Theology* (2004), *On Liturgical Asceticism* (2013), and Consecrating the World: *On Mundane Theology* (2016).

original and intended condition is inherently priestly. Human nature is oriented towards God in gratitude, praise, obedience, and thanksgiving.

The priestly existence of the human person was severely altered and disfigured with the fall of Adam and Eve. Their loss of trust in God as their loving Creator not only shattered their communion with Him, it also permanently damaged their relationship with each other, as well as with the realm of nature. Suspicion, control, lust, and possessiveness disturbed their nuptial relations. A spirit of craving, manipulation, calculation, and utilitarianism replaced their priestly perception of the world. Instead of appearing as a gift from God, communicating and drawing them into deeper intimacy with Him, created beauty now appeared as a collection of "things" to be taken, possessed, and used as ends in themselves. The connection between gift and Giver was severed. The world now appeared to have an existence of its own. "Objects" in the world now seemed to be cut off from the giftedness and co-inherence with the Creator they previously enjoyed.

A false sense of autonomy also entered creation. Adam and Eve now experienced themselves as "on their own." They were forced to leave Paradise and to engage in a world that now seemed to "run itself." Harsh and unforgiving "laws of nature" replaced theophanic *ethos* of the Garden. What previously was resplendent with the glory of God now seemed devoid of His divine presence. *Homo adorans* suddenly became *homo laborans*: man who labors. Whereas life in the Original Unity had been a liturgy of perpetual adoration, it now became an on-going battle simply to eek out a living. It became a conflict and source of misunderstanding and confusion, one in which woman would seek to control man, and man would seek to possess woman (Gen. 3:16). *Eros* was quickly deteriorating into erotica.

It is significant, in this context, that our first parents' original sin involved *eating*. Prior to their fall from communion with God, their hunger had been for Him alone, not for the fruits of creation. Following their sin, however, their hunger became disordered and misdirected. They hunger now for the *things* of God rather than for God Himself. Creation becomes an *unsatisfying surrogate* for the Source and Fulfillment of their deepest desires. Their desire for God was projected onto things that are not God. Eating became an instrument and image of self-satisfaction and isolation. Voraciousness replaced veneration as the human *modus operands*. Craving and consumption crowded out reverence and respect in the human psyche. The world no longer served as God intended it, namely as a means of thanksgiving and communion with Himself. Instead, it became an end in itself, to be pursued and plundered, possessed and manipulated, in ways foreign to God's plan and in manner destructive of the persons who approach it in this fashion. A mechanistic and utilitarian attitude replaces a eucharistic disposition as the defining characteristic of fallen human persons.

*Religion*, as a human construct, also appears for the first time in a world separated from God. "*Religio*" functions as a replacement for the priestly *adoratio* that came naturally in the Garden of Eden. Religion, ritual, cult, and rite emerge within the fallen human community as substitutes for the unmediated communion with God enjoyed by our first parents in the original unity. Priesthood and sacrifice develop as *institutional surrogates* for *inherent inclinations of praise and thanksgiving* that originally defined the eucharistic make-up of Adam and Eve.

It is significant that the early Christians were accused of being "atheists" and "cannibals" in their worship. They were called atheists because they were said to exhibit a "freedom from cult" uncharacteristic of other religions. There were accused of being cannibals because it was rumored that they consumed the flesh and blood of the very God they worshipped. Both of these indictments were, in their own ways, correct. Christians of the early church certainly believed Christianity to be the *end of religion* as the fallen world understood it. They saw their own "*leitourgia*" (worship) as replacing all systems of pre-Christian and pagan worship. What Adam and Eve lost through the Fall, they saw Jesus Christ restoring through His Redemptive Sacrifice. With the coming of Christ, the world regained its being as an instrument and sacrament of *communio* with the Triune God. Life is now returned to fallen man as the ordinary means of divine transformation. The very things of creation became again sacraments of *schesis* (intimate relationship) with the Creator. Mere water became a means of deification in the mystery (*mysterion, sacramentum*) of Baptism. Simple bread and wine became the mystical instruments of participation in very Body and Blood of Jesus. Man is once again united in ecstatic communion with God, without needing to abscond from the materiality of His own, good creation. Human persons can achieve intimacy with their Creator and Redeemer using ordinary goods of the earth, no longer needing to seek out pagan or occultist practices to manipulate the moods of the gods.

In Christ and His (sacramental) Mysteries, the Trinity returns the world to the very creatures who defaced it. Creation is given back to them as a redeemed, restored, recapitulated gift of His love. Through the power of the Holy Spirit, the simple materials of God's earth become the means of the world's re-creation, first in the sacred humanity of Jesus' Incarnation, then in the sacred mysteries of the Christian *koinonia* (community). In and through the Person and actions of Christ, God re-makes the world into a divinely restored venue for the re-entry of fallen humanity into perfect unity with the Most Blessed Trinity.

# THE WELLSPRING OF WORSHIP[121]

*Leitourgia* (Liturgy) is what humans do to participate in the divine liturgy of heaven. In the grace and power of what the early church called, simply, "the Mysteries," we are privileged to enter into the heavenly liturgy, the Wedding Feast of the Lamb (Rev. 19:7-9). This is what Fr. Jean Corbon calls "the fontal liturgy:" "the Mystery kept hidden through all ages" (Eph. 3:9), revealed now in the Person of Jesus and extended to us in His Mystical Body, the Church (*Ekklesia*). Entering into the Eucharistic *Synaxis* (Assembly), we are *taken up into* the heavenly liturgy. This Divine Liturgy has been going on from all eternity. There, Jesus, the Great High Priest "lives to make eternal intercession for us" (Heb. 7:25). Through our Baptism into Christ, we are given a share in His priesthood, enabling us to join in the *perichoresis* (ecstatic love and joy) and *parrhesia* (bold confidence) Jesus experiences within the life of the Trinity as celebrant of the heavenly liturgy.

As eternal High Priest, Jesus stands ever before the Father in praise and thanksgiving as His "only begotten Son." He lives also "to make intercession for sinners" (Heb. 7:25; Rom. 8:34). Yet, this intercession on our behalf is an extension of His more fontal (original, foundational, inner-Trinitarian) identity as the eternally grateful (eucharistic) Son of the Father. He offers perpetual "sacrifices of praise" to the Father Who eternally begets Him. He gives unending thanksgiving to the Father from whom He "proceeds." He is ever mindful of the fact that "all that the Father has He has given me" (Jn. 16:15). He returns all to the Father as an expression of His gratitude and His love. Priesthood and

---

[121] The following section is inspired and informed by Jean Corbon's brilliant presentation of the Divine Liturgy in his book by the same title, *The Wellspring of Worship* (San Francisco: Ignatius Press, 2005).

177

Eucharist define the identity of Christ, not only as mediator between us and the Father, but also in His primordial relationship with the Father as God's only begotten Son.

The Wedding Feast of the Lamb (Rev. 19:7-9) is the eschatological fulfillment of the fontal liturgy within the Trinity. Under the direction of Jesus, the Great High Priest, the heavenly Supper of the Lamb also includes those "predestined from the foundation of the world to be holy and blameless in His sight" (Eph. 1:4). Jesus is Alpha and Omega (Rev. 1:17). As Omega, He is revealed in heaven "as a Lamb standing, as though it had been slain" (Rev. 5:6). Gathered around Him are all those who have been assimilated into His own heavenly worship. *Anagogically* (eschatologically), we are gathered into Jesus at the End of history in a way that mirrors and extends our incorporation into Him as the 2$^{nd}$ Adam in our Baptism. It also fulfills and completes our corporate membership in the 1$^{st}$ Adam at the time of our creation.

The truth of who we are as persons is unveiled, fulfilled, perfected, and fully defined, only in the Wedding Feast of the Lamb. At the eschatological banquet, God gives each of us "a white stone, with a new name written on the stone which no one knows except him who receives it" (Rev. 2:17). The names and faces intended for us by God from all eternity – our true identities - are disclosed to us only in the heavenly Victory celebration of the Lamb who was slain.

This same mystery is made present as we participate in the earthly liturgy of the Christian *synaxis* (Assembly). The mystery of the Eucharist is the historical embodiment of, and the portal into, the Wedding Feast of the Lamb. Just as the Paschal Mystery of Christ, though a once-only historical event, is also eternally present, infusing all of history with its Presence and power, so too, the Wedding Feast of the Lamb, though essentially an eschatological event, manifests itself in the Eucharistic Liturgy of the Church. Going to Mass is, quite literally, entering heaven, just as "being baptized" is, truly and ontologically, entering into the death and resurrection of Christ. These are no mere metaphors. They are central mysteries of our Faith, the source and summit of our lives in Jesus Christ.

Contemplating the *Ascension* of Christ enables us even more powerfully to apprehend the co-inherence of the divine and earthly liturgies. "When I am lifted up," Jesus says, "I will draw all men to myself" (Jn. 3:14). "God, who is rich in mercy...has raised us up with Christ and made us sit with Him in the heavenly places...(Eph. 2:6). In Christ we are *already seated* at the right hand of the Father. Those of us baptized into Christ have been inserted, as it were, not only into His death and resurrection, but also into His Ascension. We have ascended with Him. There, at the right hand of the Father, we live and reign with Him, integral to His identity as Great High Priest.

The Ascension of Jesus will be fully complete only when all those "predestined from the foundation of the world" have been incorporated into His glorified Body, the Church. It is no accident that many ancient Christian churches have icons of Christ's Ascension in the domes of their basilicas. As the Christian *synaxis* gathers beneath them, it is as if the Lord Jesus elevates the Assembly into His own Ascension. Through His Ascension, the risen Christ mystically draws all who seek Him into the magnetic *communio* of Father, Son, and Holy Spirit. The icon of Jesus in His Ascension serves as a sacramental sign of how the risen Christ unites His faithful adorers into His own priestly worship of the Father in the bosom of the Trinity. This process will continue "until we all... form the perfect Man who is Christ come to full stature" (Eph. 4:13).

It is impossible to overestimate the union Christ establishes between heaven and earth in the sacrament of the Eucharist. "All that was in Christ Jesus," St. Pope Leo the Great said, "has passed over into His Mysteries."[122] In the Eucharistic liturgy, Jesus raises the world into the glory of God. He also brings the heavenly liturgy down upon the earth. Through the power of the Holy Spirit, the Wedding Feast of the Lamb, like the Old Testament *Shekinah* (Ex. 16:10; 19:9), descends upon the world to envelop and encompass those He has called out of the world (Jn. 17:16) to enter the glory of God. In the Eucharist, Jesus catches up into Himself the chosen people He has adopted for His Father. He engrafts His elect into His own priestly glorification of His Father.

---

[122] *Sermons* 74, 2 PL 54 398A, quoted by Azkoul, *Ye Are Gods*, 13. Cited also in CCC #1114.

The High Priestly prayer of Jesus becomes our own. Or, better: we become an integral part of His infinitely salvific prayer as our Eternal High Priest.

Nothing about the earthly liturgy or the sacramental economy given us by Christ can be adequately appreciated or understood without prolonged contemplation of the fontal and heavenly liturgies. As the *Catechism of the Catholic Church* reminds us, the liturgy is a work of the Most Blessed Trinity (#1077-1134). Only very derivatively is the liturgy a human action. The Divine Liturgy is *God's* incorporation of human persons into the primordial liturgy of the Trinitarian Persons within their own divine communion. We "participate" in the heavenly liturgy of Christ by allowing ourselves to be taken up into its glory. "Active participation" in the liturgy is not something we effect by busying ourselves with liturgical ministries; it is, rather, a more contemplative matter of allowing ourselves to be drawn into the Memorial Prayer of Christ as He re-presents His Paschal Sacrifice to the Father on our behalf.

"Liturgy is also an 'action' of the whole Christ (*Christus totus*)."[123] The worship in heaven forms the basis, and supplies the power, for the earthly liturgy. "In the earthly liturgy we have a foretaste of that heavenly liturgy which is [eternally] celebrated in the Holy City of Jerusalem...where Christ is sitting at the right hand of God..."[124] What we experience as a foretaste on earth, the saints experience in its fullness in heaven. The eternal liturgy precedes and makes possible all our earthly exercises of worship. "It is in this eternal liturgy that the Spirit and the Church enable us to participate whenever we celebrate the mystery of salvation in the sacraments."[125] "In the [earthly] liturgy, it is his own Paschal Mystery [Passover] that Christ...makes present."[126]

We can see from these seminal passages of the *Catechism of the Catholic Church* that the earthly liturgy manifests and conveys the heavenly

---

[123] *Catechism of the Catholic Church*, #1136
[124] *Catechism of the Catholic Church* #1090
[125] *Catechism of the Catholic Church* #1139
[126] *Catechism of the Catholic Church* #1084

action of Jesus Christ. He alone is the Priest at every celebration of the Eucharist. Further, in the liturgy Christ is still in the process of "drawing all things to Himself" (Jn. 12:32). He does so, as priest, in order to re-present the world, whole and restored, back to the Father. "As often [therefore] as the liturgy is celebrated, the work of our salvation is carried out."[127] This is why the *Catechism* insists that the Eucharist is the "source and summit" upon which Christ brings to completion what He has already accomplished for our Redemption.

Once we realize that the Ascension of Jesus is the return of the Incarnate Word to the heart of the Father (Jn. 3:13; 6:62; Eph. 4:10), having accomplished his mission of redemption (cf. Is. 55:11), we can see how the liturgy fulfills the ultimate meaning of Jesus' promise, "when I am lifted up I will draw all men to myself" (Jn.12:32; cf. 3:14; 8:28). Jesus is referring here not only to His being lifted up in His Crucifixion but also to His Ascension. In His Ascension Jesus brings with Him to the Father all those who are initiated into Him through the liturgical Mysteries.

He bequeaths us the sacramental Mysteries precisely for this purpose. The heavenly liturgy celebrates the Son's return to His Father's House, a return which now includes all of God's prodigal children, gathered into the Savior through His sacramental mysteries. All is not yet finished; but, the great event of history – Jesus' Paschal Mystery – and all those who have received a share in this Mystery through their initiation into Christ are now placed in the heart of the Trinity. There, one with the Father, in the power and glory of the Holy Spirit, the Wedding Feast of the Lamb, already begun, is brought to completion through the continual addition of those who have been called into this Divine *Synaxis*. Assembled as a single body in the earthly liturgy, we participate now in the Life of the Trinity through our Eucharistic union with the Lamb who was slain.

---

[127] *Catechism of the Catholic Church* #1364

# EUCHARIST

*It* is now time for us to enter more deeply into a contemplative vision of the Eucharist. Unless our minds and hearts are illumined by a mystical grace from the Holy Spirit, we will be unable to appreciate the more personalist, Trinitarian dimensions of this unfathomable mystery.

The Eucharist is our quintessential participation in the fontal liturgy of Father, Son, and Holy Spirit. More specifically, it is our incorporation into the priestly service offered to the Father by the Son through the power of the Holy Spirit. The Eucharist is the eternal Sabbath made present. It is a perpetual epiphany on earth of the unending heavenly banquet. It is the end of history made present in time and space to those who called to the table of the Lord. It is a gift of divine election culminating in the deification of the members of Christ's Body when they gather as the *synaxis* of the Lord.

In the Eucharist, the Kingdom of God appears in our midst. It is the ultimate theophany. It is the Light of Tabor displayed and refracted throughout the world. The "end of the world" is made present in the Eucharist in a veiled fullness. The Eucharistic Sacrifice constitutes the perpetual memorial of the Lord's Paschal, His priestly offering of praise to the Father. In this holy Passover, we are assimilated into the Easter mysteries, thereby entering into the $8^{th}$ Day of His unending, resurrected Life. All of human time and space is gathered up and divinized each and every time the Holy Mysteries are carried out.

The *Ecclesia* is the communion of saints gathered around the Throne of the Lamb Who is slain (Rev. 5:6). We experience here an anticipated fullness of the glory and power of the Kingdom yet to come. The world to come is revealed in anticipation in the Eucharist through the power of the Holy Spirit. "Remembering the future,"[128] we enter into the eschatological fullness of our union with the Trinity within the constraints of time and space. Our participation in the Christian *Leitourgia* is a real entrance into the Day that has no evening. All of eternity is made present wherever the Eucharistic Sacrifice of Praise is enacted.

The Eucharist, then, is the "sacrament" of the world to come. "Sacrament," in English, conveys little of the power and majesty of the Greek term for Mystery, *Mysterion*. The Eucharist is the *Mysterion* of Christ Paschal Sacrifice. "In the liturgy of the Church, it is principally his own Paschal mystery that Christ signifies and makes present."[129] As often as the Eucharistic liturgy "is celebrated on the altar, the work of our redemption is carried out."[130] "Sacrament," viewed in an overly-linear manner, tends to short-circuit and neutralize what serves in a more majestic way to communicate, not just the mental memory of the events of our salvation, but their Trinitarian form and content.

"Celebration" is another word used to describe the action taking place in the Christian *leitourgia* that often devalues our appreciation of the Eucharistic *Mysterion*. The Eucharistic Mystery is of a piece with "The Mystery kept hidden through all the ages" (Eph. 3:9). God's "plan [is]...to unite all things in Christ, things in heaven and on earth" (Eph. 1:10). This plan, "kept hidden for generations in God who created all things" is now "made manifest" both to "the powers and principalities" who have opposed it from the beginning of time, as well as to those "chosen in Him before the foundation of the world

---

[128] The *anaphora* of the Liturgy of St. John Chrysostom remembers the future as realized in the present when the priest prays, "Remembering, therefore, this salutary commandment [to "Do this as the Memorial of Me"], and all that was done for us: the cross, the tomb, the resurrection on the third day, the ascension into heaven, the sitting at the right hand, and *the second and glorious coming*, we offer to You, Yours of Your own on behalf of all and for all" (emphasis added). This prayer conveys the sense of the eschatological reality of Christ's Second Coming made present, yet not identical with, the Eucharistic action.

[129] *Catechism of the Catholic Church* #1085.

[130] *Catechism of the Catholic Church* # *1364, LG 3;* cf. 1 Cor. 5:7.

to be holy and blameless in his sight" (Eph. 3:10; 1:4). The Eucharistic *Mysterion*, therefore, is an extension of the "hidden wisdom of God. It is a making visible of that which God decreed before the ages for our glorification" (1 Cor. 2:7). To speak of the Eucharist as *something* we *"celebrate"* is to subjectivize a *Mysterion*. It easily obscures the fact that in the Eucharist, we are taken up into a far vaster Mystery than human activity can comprehend. While technically accurate, the term *celebration* conveys little of the Mystery of God's hidden Wisdom that is being displayed and conveyed in the Eucharistic Sacrifice.

We critique the terms "sacrament," and "celebration" only to strengthen our appreciation of the Eucharistic *Mysterion*. We need to re-acquire the deep and profound liturgical sense that characterized our ancient tradition. Beginning with St. Paul, the Church has always understood the Eucharistic Mystery to be the cornerstone of God's all-embracing plan of salvation. This plan issues from His eternal Wisdom, active before the foundation of the world (Wis. 9:9-11). "In the fullness of time" (Eph. 1:10), our salvation was accomplished through the Paschal Mystery of the historical person of Jesus Christ. This Mystery of our Redemption is communicated to us throughout the ages in the Eucharistic *Mysterion* of the *Ecclesia Catholica*. All of salvation history is recapitulated and perfected every time the Christian *synaxis* gathers for the divine action of the Holy Eucharist.

We must never forget that the Eucharistic *Mysterion* is the very Person of Jesus Christ. In the Eucharistic *Leitourgia*, Jesus is actively gathering to Himself, through the power of the Holy Spirit, all those "predestined from the foundation of the world" to be "recapitulated" in Him and re-presented to the Father. "All that was in Christ," to repeat the important words of St. Pope Leo the Great, "has passed over into His Mysteries."[131] We must not tarnish this vision of the "Sacred Mysteries" by conceiving of the liturgy merely as something "we celebrate" or view this or any of the sacramental Mysteries as "things" simply "instituted by Christ to give grace."

This leads us, briefly, to a discussion of the meaning of the phrase,

---

[131] Pope St. Leo the Great, *Sermon* 74, 2 PL 54 398A, cited in Azkoul, *Ye Are Gods*, 13.

"the Real Presence" of Jesus in the Eucharist. Ironically, a misdirected emphasis on transubstantiation can undermine our appreciation of the Eucharist as God's chosen instrument for our deification and the world's restoration as a "new creation in Christ" (2 Cor. 5:17; cf. Rom. 8:22). One liturgical theologian has called transubstantiation "the suicide of sacramental theology."[132] This hyperbolic claim is certainly not because we don't believe in transubstantiation. We most assuredly do. It is the bedrock and unquestioned consensus of the early church.[133] But like the term "symbol" to which our belief in "the Real Presence" is often opposed, the concept of "transubstantiation" can fail to convey the deifying and redemptive *action* taking place in the Eucharistic *Mysterion*. Entering into the Eucharist is entering into an *active encounter* with the *Person* of Jesus. A static or materialist understanding of the term "transubstantiation" can obscure the essentially dynamic and personalist character of this divine and transformative encounter.

Historically speaking, the concept of transubstantiation became necessary only when the patristic understanding of "Symbol" had broken apart. The Fathers of the Church knew of no distinction or difference between the "Symbols" of the Faith and the "sacraments" of the Church. They were the very same Mysteries. Thus, St. Maximus the Confessor, the sacramental theologian *par excellence* of the patristic age, calls the Body and Blood of Christ in the Eucharist symbols (*"symbola"*), images (*"apeikonismata"*), and mysteries (*"mysteria"*).[134] "Symbol," as used by Maximus and other Fathers of the Church, is in no way in opposed to what is "real." The "really real" (i.e., Trinitarian Life) is *communicated* to fallen humanity in and through the "Showings Forth" in "Mysterious Form" of the "Holy Things." "Holy Things for Holy People!" is what the priest declares before distributing Communion in the Byzantine Rite. These "Holy Things" are "symbols" of the divine reality they contain and communicate. Precisely as "Symbols," they

---

[132] Schmemann, *For the Life of the World*, 144

[133] See Casmir A. Kucharek, *The Sacramental Mysteries: A Byzantine Approach* (Allendale, NJ: Alleluia Press, 1976) 156-174.

[134] Schmemann, ibid., 139.

partake of, and participate in, the very *Mysterion* of God's Trinitarian Exchange. They are one with the Divine Life that they convey and effect. Opposing "sacraments" as "efficacious signs," to "symbols," therefore, is a mistake. It represents a false dichotomy unknown in the early Church. The trivialization of Catholic sacramental theology in the 21st century is both a result and a reflection of this tragic loss of the patristic appreciation of the Mystery of the Symbol.

An even greater factor in the sad ossification of the Catholic sacramental tradition stems from the loss of the felt sense of the Divine Liturgy as a *theandric action*.[135] A *theandric* action is an action performed by Christ working both as God and man. In the Eucharist, Jesus uses the instrumentality of his human body and blood to communicate to us a share in His divine nature. It is in the Eucharist that we most assuredly become "partakers of the divine nature" (2 Pt. 1:4). This goes to the heart of the matter. The Eucharist is primarily an *action*. It is not the presentation of a *something*, either for our instruction, edification, or our consumption. In the Eucharist we are "taken up into" the intimate life of the Trinity. It is a movement of ascension and assumption, of assimilation and participation. We are given "a share in" the divine priesthood of Jesus Christ. We are inserted by the Holy Spirit into His heavenly intercession before the Father as our Great High Priest (Heb. 7:24-25). Jesus lives forever to make intercession for us (cf. Rom. 8:34).

It is important to recall, as the *Catechism of the Catholic Church* makes clear, that the liturgy is the work of the *entire Holy Trinity*.[136] The Father is the *Source and Goal* of the liturgy. The Son is the one-only High *Priest* in the liturgy, making a memorial offering of Himself to the Father. And the Holy Spirit is the real *"Celebrant"* of the liturgy, preparing us for, recalling to us, and making present for us, "the Lamb Who was slain." The entire drama of our salvation, as well as our incorporation into it, is made present in the sacramental enactment of Christ's Paschal Mystery.

It is easy to forget who the main Actors in the Divine Liturgy are when the liturgy is presented as essentially a human construction

---

[135] *Catechism of the Catholic Church* # 257-260
[136] *Catechism of the Catholic Church* # 1077-1112

in which we are supposed to "actively participate." This approach betrays a misunderstanding both of liturgical "action" and deifying "participation." Human "participation" in the Eucharistic Mystery means to "receive a share in," or "partake of," the redemptive *work of Jesus*. This work is "made present and carried out" in the liturgical celebration. We are taken up into the Person and mission of Jesus through our "participation" in the Eucharistic Liturgy.

It is the apogee of our faith to realize that through the outpouring of the Holy Spirit at Pentecost, humankind is now capacitated for and invited into the Divine Economy through this Trinitarian Liturgy. The historical "work" of Jesus' Paschal Mystery is now, in a "new dispensation," communicated to us through the liturgy for "the life of the world." The work of Christ on the Cross, in the tomb, risen from the tomb, and ascended into heaven is made present in the "public work" ("liturgy") of the Church. We are mysteriously and miraculously given a share in His redemptive Sacrifice. Through our "participation" in the liturgy, we become "partakers of the divine nature" (2 Pt. 1:4). We are deified through our association with Christ Sacrifice, yet it remains forever His liturgy unto the Father, not ours. *He* re-presents His saving Sacrifice to the Father in the Divine Liturgy; through the power of His Holy Spirit. *He* incorporates us into it. The liturgy is an action of the whole Christ (*Christus totus*),[137] but it is always Jesus who serves as the Priest. The Father is always the Source and Goal of the liturgy, and the Holy Spirit is He who makes saving Paschal Mystery present and mystically makes us part of Christ's own Self Offering.

It is a symptom of the deterioration of sacramental theology and liturgical spirituality that we have lost sight of the fact that the liturgy of the New Covenant is the Person of Jesus Christ Himself. We have forgotten that *He is still acting and interceding on our behalf* in the "work" (liturgy). We have difficulty seeing that the liturgy is not a "something," but a "Someone." In the Eucharist Jesus is exercising His eternal High Priesthood in the presence of His Father for the salvation of the world.

---

[137] *Catechism of the Catholic Church* # 1136.

Through the power of the Holy Spirit, we are made one with His Person and His work.

The Eucharist may be described as "the real presence" of Christ, not primarily because He is substantially contained in the instrumental species under the appearance of bread and wine, but because "participation" in the Eucharist is a real, personal encounter with the *Hypostasis* of Our Savior. We meet Him in the Eucharist acting as the Great High Priest, re-presenting Himself in memorial before the Father on our behalf. He invites us to be one with Him in His loving act of eternal intercession, praise, and thanksgiving. He gives us a share in His eternal High Priesthood. Our "participation" in the liturgy is an expression and enactment of our experiential relationship with the Trinity, and with one another, in Christ, through power of the Holy Spirit.

In this light we can see more easily how the liturgy does not simply commemorate a past event. It *makes present* the Divine Person of Jesus, together with His Redemptive Sacrifice and eternal, theandric intercession on our behalf. Through the power of His Holy Spirit, we assimilated into His Sacrifice and made an integral part of His perpetual Offering of Himself to His Father. In the Eucharist, we can say Jesus offers us in Himself on behalf of us. Jesus is never *extrinsic* to our worship; we are now forever *intrinsic* to His. He is the head, we the members. This symbiotic mystery never ends. Engrafting us to Himself in Baptism, He now offers us together with Himself forever in His Memorial Sacrifice. His Father remains eternally the Source and Goal of this Offering. Their Holy Spirit is the Power through which the Mystery forever takes place.

The liturgy, therefore, is never something we do either "in (mental) memory" of Jesus or somehow "alongside of" Jesus, present on the altar. Jesus Himself is always the Great High Priest in every liturgy. He incorporates us into the memorial re-presentation of His Paschal Sacrifice as we gather around Him as His Mystical Body. We are his divinely assembled *synaxis*, both worshipping and one with the Lamb Who is slain. From start to finish Jesus is the Priest acting on our behalf. In the liturgy the work of our redemption is made present and carried out. It is His action into which we are drawn and given a share. We are participants in His priesthood, perfectly fulfilling the ancient promise, "you shall be unto me a kingdom of priests, a holy nation, a people set apart" (Ex. 19:6; cf. Isa. 61:6; 1 Pt. 2:5, 9). Our identity as *homo adorans* is brought to completion in Jesus, our Great High Priest, as He incorporates us into His own divine Priesthood through our participation in His Eucharistic Memorial.

*Section Three*

# *Ecclesia: The Sacrament of Deification*

# ECCLESIA DE EUCHARISTIA

*F*rom all that has been said about the deifying power of the liturgy, we can easily see why the *Corpus Mysticum* of the Eucharist is called "the source and summit of the Christian life" (CCC #1324). It is the beginning and end of our life "in Christ." At the same time, the Eucharist creates another great mystery in which our personal *theosis* finds its final purpose and fulfillment. This mystery is the mystery of the Church. The ultimate creation of the Eucharistic Memorial is what Pope John Paul II sagaciously termed *"Ecclesia de Eucharistia,"* the Church *of* the Eucharist. *The Church,* as the Mystical Body of Christ, is the final purpose and ultimate term of Jesus' *Corpus Mysticum* that He gives us in the Eucharist. *The Eucharist makes the Church.*[138]

Popes John Paul II and Benedict XVI have strongly promoted what has been termed "Eucharistic Ecclesiology." In this, they are indebted to their *ressourcement* mentor, Henri de Lubac, who, as noted earlier, examines in detail the patristic understanding of the term *Corpus Mysticum* (Mystical Body of Christ). For the first nine centuries of the Church, de Lubac says, the term *Corpus Mysticum* (Mystical Body of Christ) referred to the *Eucharistic* Body of Christ. Only later did it come to refer to the *Ecclesial* Body of Christ (the Church). Throughout all of Christian history, however, the Eucharistic Body of Christ is understood to be given *for the creation and realization of* the *Ecclesial* Body of Christ. The *Corpus Mysticum* of the Eucharist culminates in the *Corpus Mysticum* of the Church. The Church is thus being built up into

---

[138] This is the leading insight and emphasis of the *ressourcement* theologians, including Henri de Lubac, Hans Urs von Balthasar, and Joseph Ratzinger, that led in part to the emphasis in Vatican II to the renewal of the liturgy and its emphasis on what has become known as *Communio* Ecclesiology.

the *Christus Totus*, the Total Christ. Jesus, Head and members, is knit together into a final *pleroma* (fullness) through the celebration of the Eucharist.

Prior to becoming Pope, Joseph Cardinal Ratzinger wrote, "The Church *came into being* when the Lord had given his body and blood under the forms of bread and wine...[and] [T]he Church is built up from the eucharistic meal...the whole purpose of the Eucharist is to gather people into the Body of the Lord...so as to transform them into the living Body of Christ..."[139] The implications of this way of imagining the relationship of *Eucharistia* to *Ecclesia* require a revolution in our theological thinking. From this perspective, it is no longer possible to conceive of the Church as either ancillary or preliminary to the celebration of the Eucharist. It is *in the celebration of the Eucharist* that the Body of Christ *realizes itself* most fully. The Eucharist is the supreme *actualization* of the Church itself. It is the *manifestation* of our salvation, and the actual in-gathering of God's elect into it. The Eucharistic *Liturgia* is the *theandric* action whereby Christ incorporates those he has chosen into his resurrected and ascended Person. The Eucharistic Sacrifice is the public display and divine instrument of this mystical communion.

The Church, therefore, is not best understood an organization. It is not primarily an ecclesial institution that contains and dispenses the Eucharist. It is better described as the mystical *event* in which the Mystical Body of Christ is actualized and manifested. Our view of the Church is severely shortchanged and skewed if we perceive it primarily as an institution that has sacraments. A more contemplative approach to the mystery of the *Ecclesia* sees the Church as the primordial Sacrament of God's *communio*. Only as a by-product of its Trinitarian activity, does it also happen to have institutions.

This way of thinking can be difficult for those who think of either

---

[139] Joseph Cardinal Ratzinger, *Called to Communion: Understanding the Church Today* (San Francisco: Ignatius Press, 1996) 75; "Einleitung zur Dogmatischen Konstitution uber de gottliche Offenbarung," cited by Maximilian Heinrich Heim, *Joseph Ratzinger: Life in the Church and Living Theology: Fundamentals of Ecclesiology with Reference to Lumen Gentium* (San Francisco: Ignatius Press, 2007) 271 (emphasis added).

the Eucharist or the Church in non-personalist ways. Neither the Eucharist nor the *Ecclesia* can be regarded simply as "things." Both are *the very Person* of Jesus, in His *Corpus Tri-forme*, drawing fallen, yet chosen, persons into His own divine Mystery. The celebration of the Eucharist is always an *eschatological* event, as well as a *mystical* encounter with the risen and ascended Lord. As an eschatological event and a personal encounter, the celebration of the Eucharist "brings into being" something that did not exist apart from the action of the liturgy.

What, we may ask, could possibly be "added" to the world or to the believer, much less to God, that was not fully realized before the Eucharist caused it to be? It sounds like heresy to say something could be "added to" or "wanting for" God. Recall, however, that in His divinity, Jesus is a *Corporate* Person. He is described by St. Paul as possessing a "Mystical Body" (Rom. 12:4-5; 1 Cor. 12:12; Eph. 4:14-16; Col. 3:14). This is because, as Paul himself discovered during his conversion (Acts 19), *Jesus is never not Himself without those He has predestined to comprise His members.*

We return here to the paradoxical double negatives that seem always to be necessary when seeking to come to grips with the seamless mysteries of the Trinity, Incarnation, and *Economia* of Salvation. Jesus is a *Mystical Person* who unique identity as Son of God and Son of Man means that He is never separated from His Father and the Holy Spirit above, nor from the members of His Mystical Body below. Facing heavenward, Jesus is never fully Who He is, even as Eternal Word, apart from *communio* with the Father and the Spirit . And, looking downward, Jesus is never fully Who He is apart from inseparable *communio* with those He has called and chosen to "complete" Himself as members of His very own Body. His *Ecclesia* is His earthly *communio*. His Body, which He gives us in the Eucharist, is given for the purpose, and as the means, of knitting, binding, engrafting, and indissolubly incorporating those who receive Him into His ecclesial Body. His Mystical Body, the Church, constitutes Him as "Christ coming to full stature" (Col. 1:24, 28; 2:19). These upwards and downwards relationships of Christ are not tangential to His identity, either as man or as God.

Such holy audacity in our thinking is confirmed by the writings of the saints. St. Therese of Lisieux, Doctor of the Church, for example, often said that though, strictly speaking, God has no need of us to do anything, He chooses, in fact, never to do anything without us. This "chosen dependence" of Jesus on the persons of the *Ecclesia* to constitute His *Corpus Mysticum* reveals itself as perhaps the deepest mystery and most mystical implication of the truth that "the Eucharist makes the Church."

How are we to appreciate the mystery that Jesus, as a divine Person, incorporates countless human persons, body and soul, into His very being both as God and as man? We must, as the saints remind us, always focus on His Incarnation. In particular we must contemplate His Passion and Death (1 Cor. 1:18-2:5).[140] His Cross and His sacred humanity are now and forever the "instruments" of our incorporation into Him. Hence, our divinization in Christ always assumes a crucified and Eucharistic form. It is precisely our non-deified human understanding that makes it difficult us to grasp St. Paul's mystical language about the Body of Christ as being anything other than a metaphorical analogy to Jesus' humanity. This is a fundamental mistake, preventing us from developing a more contemplative understanding of the *Corpus Tri-forme* of the Corporate Person of Christ. To say, not only that "Jesus includes us" in His Mystical Body through the sacraments of Baptism and Eucharist, but that we are "incorporated into Christ" such as to be indispensable to Jesus in His identity as *Totus Christus*, God and man: this is the measure, challenge, and resulting belief of persons who have been transfigured and deified by the very Jesus who "desires and needs" them to bring Himself to "full stature" (Eph. 4:13).

We will not have grasped these astounding truths until we can say with sincerity that the *Corpus Mysticum* of the *Church* is no less the real, transubstantiated Person of Jesus Christ than is the *Corpus Mysticum* of Jesus in the Eucharist. The Mystical Body of Christ known

---

[140] A favorite theme of St. Teresa of Avila and St. John of the Cross, reminding us that no matter how mystical our contemplation of God becomes, it is always and irrevocably rooted in meditation upon the Incarnation and Passion of Jesus. See Thomas Dubay, S.M., *Fire Within: St. Teresa of Avila, St. John of the Cross, and the Gospel—On Prayer* (San Francisco: Ignatius Press, 1989) 217-220.

as "the Church" is a "people set apart," transubstantiated "into Christ" through participation in His actual Presence in the Mystery of the Eucharist. Jesus *indwells* His Mystical Body, the Church, in a manner equally "real" to the way in which He indwells the Eucharist. Both of these "indwellings" flow from and mirror the interpenetration of his divine and human natures in Christ's hypostatic union, as well as His perichoretic indwelling of the Father and the Holy Spirit in the life of the Trinity.

Have we understood these mystical equivalences? If "the Eucharist makes the Church," then we, as the "chosen people of God" constitute the total Person of Christ (*Christus Totus*). Our union with Christ in the Church is mysteriously equal in identity with Christ's Presence and union with us in the Eucharist. Through our participation in His Eucharistic *Corpus Mysticum*, we are changed into His Ecclesial *Corpus Mysticum*. We are transubstantiated into His ecclesial Body through reception of His transubstantiated Body and Blood in the Eucharist.

Our use of the term "transubstantiation" here returns us to a personalistic understanding of the concepts of substance and being. The primary miracle of the Eucharist is the change of persons (us) into Person (Jesus). The Mystery of the Eucharist certainly transforms bread and wine into the Body and Blood of Christ. More importantly, it also incorporates us into the Corporate (Mystical) Person of Jesus. The former is the sacramental *means* to the latter. The ultimate purpose of the institution of the Eucharist is the creation of the Church.

A personalist perspective is crucial when contemplating the changes that take place in the mystery of the Eucharist. A non-personalist and un-deified paradigm of the "sacrament" of the Eucharist portrays a human individual "receiving" the transubstantiated Body and Blood of Christ as a means of obtaining "grace" leading to "eternal salvation." As Pope Benedict XVI has written, "The concept of sacraments as the means of a grace that I receive like a supernatural medicine in order, as it were, to ensure only my own private eternal health is the supreme misunderstanding of what a sacrament truly is."[141] A more personalist, patristic, mystical, and divinized appreciation of the mystery perceives the Eucharist as the action of the Trinity incorporating – or "transubstantiating" – the recipients of His Eucharistic *Corpus Mysticum* into His ecclesial *Corpus Mysticum*. The Trinitarian action of the *Leitourgia* builds up and brings to completion Christ's identity as *Totus Christus*, Alpha and Omega. "Holy Communion," in this sense, can be understood as a Holy Communion of *Persons*. It cannot be reduced to the reception of persons of a transubstantiated object called "the Eucharist." "Communion," in a Trinitarian perspective, is never a matter of exchanging *substances*. It is always a mystery of human persons being brought into the Person of Jesus through the reception of His Body and Blood in the *Mysterium Fidei*.

What we have been saying here can perhaps be more simply illustrated by reflecting on what it is we are doing when we receive Jesus in Holy Communion. We naively think it is *we* who are receiving Jesus into ourselves when we take the Eucharist. We imagine Him coming to "dwell within us" or, perhaps more crassly, as dissolving within us for the purpose of sanctifying our souls with grace. In addition to whatever elements of truth there may be in such images, there is a much larger miracle at work in the mystery of receiving Holy Communion. More so than we receiving Him, Jesus receives us. He assimilates us in the Eucharist into His divine Person. The Fathers of the Church make this point quite clear. St. Augustine observed, "It was if I heard Your voice from on high, [saying] 'I am the food of adults; grow and you shall eat Me. You will not then change Me into yourself...but you shall be changed into Me.'"[142] Likewise, Gregory of Nyssa states, "The body [of Christ in the Eucharist] made immortal by God, once having entered ours, transforms it, and changes it completely into itself...into its own [divine] nature." St. John Chrysostom insists, "He blends himself with

---

[141] Joseph Cardinal Ratzinger, *Principles of Catholic Theology* (San Francisco: Ignatius Press, 1987) 49.

[142] St. Augustine, *Confessions* (7, 10, 16), quoted in William A. Jurgens, *The Faith of the Early Fathers, Volume* 3 (Collegeville, MN: The Liturgical Press, 1979) #1593.

us such that we become one single entity in the way the body is joined to the head."[143] And St. Maximus the Confessor concludes, "The Eucharist transforms the faithful into itself,"[144]

These saints give voice to the patristic consensus that by receiving Christ into ourselves in the Eucharist, we are *received into Him* and assimilated into His *Corpus Mysticum*. The Eucharist is more a mystery of ascension, incorporation, and elevation of the human person into Christ, than it is an act of the condescension or dissolution of the Person of Jesus into the Christian "Participation in the Body and Blood of Christ effects nothing else but that we become that which we consume... [for] the effect of our sharing in the body and blood of Christ is to change us into what we have received."[145]

More recently, Pope Benedict XVI, carrying this patristic tradition forward in his continuing efforts at *ressourcement*, has written powerfully of the divinely assimilative power of the Eucharist:

By eating the one bread, St. Augustine says, we ourselves become what we eat...Consequently the whole process is reversed: the man who eats this bread is assimilated by it, taken into it; he is fused into this bread...it means that I myself become part of this new "bread" which he creates by transubstantiating all earthly reality...Jesus Christ opens the way to the impossible, to communion between God and man, since he, the incarnate Word, is this communion,. He performs the 'alchemy' which melts down human nature and infuses it into the being of God. To receive the Lord in the Eucharist, therefore, means entering into a community of being with Christ, it means entering through that opening in human nature through which God is accessible...Hence Communion means the fusion of existences...my 'I' is assimilated to that of Jesus, it is made similar to him in an exchange that increasingly breaks through the lines of division. This same event takes place in the

---

[143] St. John Chrysostom, *Homily on John*, 46 (PG 59,260), quoted by Olivier Clement, *The Roots of Christian Mysticism: Texts from the Patristic Era with Commentary*, 115.
[144] St. Gregory of Nyssa, *Catechetical Oration* 37 (PG 45,96), cited by Clement, ibid., 109.
[145] Pope St. Leo I, *Sermon* 63, 7, quoted in Jurgens, *The Faith of the Early Fathers*, Volume 1, #2206.

case of all who communicate; they are all assimilated to this 'bread' and thus are made one among themselves – one body. Communion makes the Church...[and] We can call it 'people of God' only because it is through communion with Christ that man gains access to a relationship with God that he cannot establish by his own power.[146]

Pope Benedict's words perfectly summarize the mystically dynamic mystery of the *Corpus Mysticum*. The Eucharist makes the Church, and the Church constitutes the Mystical Body of Christ. Jesus has bequeathed to us the Mystery of the *Ecclesia de Eucharistia* for the purpose of creating and bringing to completion His identity as the *Christus Totus*.

Jesus is always our Head, but never without us, His members. In the Eucharist, through the power of His Holy Spirit, we are organically grafted into Him (cf. Jn. 15:1-8) and formed by Him into His ecclesial Body, the Church. As the Assembly (*Synaxis*) of those incorporated into Him through the Eucharist, the *Ecclesia* is integral to the mystery of His *Corpus Mysticum*. We are ingredient to His identity as the *Christus Totus*. To love the Church is to love Jesus Himself.[147] To separate the Church from Jesus, in thought, word, or deed, is to seek to divide what God has eternally united.

---

[146] Quotes from Pope Benedict XVI found in Rev. Peter John Cameron, O.P., ed., *Benedictus: Day by Day with Pope Benedict XVI* (San Francisco: Magnificat/Ignatius Press, 2006) 191-193.

[147] See the *Catechism of the Catholic Church* #795, quoting St. Augustine ("Let us rejoice then and give thanks that we have become not only Christians, but Christ Himself... Our redeemer has shown himself to be one person with the holy Church who he has taken to himself."), Pope St. Gregory the Great ("Head and members for as it were one and the same mystical person."), and Joan of Arc ("About Jesus Christ and the Church, I simply know they're just one thing, and we shouldn't complicate the matter.").

# AN ANAGOGICAL VISION

"*I* saw the holy city, new Jerusalem, coming down out of heaven, prepared as a bride adorned for her husband...and He who sat upon the throne said, 'Behold, I make all things new...'" (Rev. 21:2, 5). The heavenly Jerusalem, the Church triumphant, is the culmination and perfection of the progressive fulfillments we see manifest throughout the drama of salvation.

The heavenly Jerusalem is Jesus Himself in His glorified fullness. "Christ has died, Christ is risen, Christ will come again!" This is our *Mystrerium Fidei*, the central Mystery of our Faith. Jesus is the Eternal Word: the One who is, the One Who was, and the One Who is to come. Christ's "multiform contemporaneity"[148] finds expression in His *tri-forme* corporeality. He is present, in His Incarnation, as Jesus of Nazareth. He is present as a *Corpus Mysticum* (Mystical Body) in His *Ecclesia de Eucharistia* (Church). His Church comes to full stature as the *Christus Totus* in what is anagogically (eschatologically) described as the heavenly Jerusalem. There Jesus reigns forever as the Lamb Who Was Slain (Rev. 5:6). He Himself is the Glory in that City where He is the only Light that is needed (Rev. 21:22). On its walls are written the names of the Lamb's Twelve Apostles (Rev. 21:14). There He rejoices with all the saints who, through Him, with Him, and in Him, are full participants in the Wedding Feast of the Lamb (Rev. 19:7-9). As integral members of His Mystical Body, "they shall reign with Him forever and ever" (Rev. 22:5).

---

[148] This felicitous phrase, used to describe Jesus' ability, as a divine Person, to be present simultaneously in the past, present and future, can be found in Boris Bobrinskoy, *The Mystery of the Trinity: Trinitarian Experience and Vision in the Biblical and Patristic Tradition* (Crestwood, NY: St. Vladimir Seminary Press, 1999) 170.

This picture of the New Jerusalem coming down from heaven is known as the *anagogical vision*.[149] *Anagogy* is the key to understanding salvation history. It is the final fulfillment of all historical anticipations. To be interpreted correctly, God's plan of salvation – the Great Mystery, as St. Paul describes it (Eph., 1:9-10) – must be read *backwards from the future*. The mysterious term *anagogy* turns our attention to the final fulfillment of the *Ecclesia de Eucharistia*. It supplies us with a vision of the trans-historical perfection of the holy *synaxis* (Assembly) that Christ creates by giving Himself to the world in the Eucharist. *Anagogy* refers to the final "recapitulation" of fallen humanity into the heavenly *Ecclesia*. It is the completion of Christ's work of redemption. Anagogically, we see the City of God, assembled around the Lamb Who Was Slain, as the final gift of the Son, delivered unto the Father for all eternity.

*Typology* is the mechanism we use to conceive of the several, interrelated forms of anticipation and fulfillment that culminate in the anagogical vision of the Wedding Feast of the Lamb (Rev. 19:7-9). The Letter to the Hebrews employs the method of typology: "In past times, God spoke in fragmentary and varied ways to our fathers through the prophets," the author begins, "but in this final age, he has spoken to us through his Son, whom he has made heir of all things and through whom he first created the universe" (Heb. 1:1-2). Jesus is the culmination and perfection of all that has gone before. Jesus replaces the Law with himself, and 'recapitulates' - fulfilling in his very Person - all the practices and aspirations of ancient Israel. Everything that came before Jesus was a *type* or "foreshadowing" (Heb. 9:5) of the mystery of salvation fulfilled in Him. Jesus is the supreme reality to which the "shadows" and prefigurations of the Old Covenant give way and find completion

In the course of Christian history, beginning with the early Church Fathers, typology developed into an elaborate and imaginative *four-fold sense of Scripture*. Henri de Lubac has shown in detail how this scheme included the literal (historical), allegorical (ecclesial), tropological

---

[149] See also my book, *Deified Vision: Towards an Anagogical Catholicism*.

(moral), anagogical (eschatological) senses of the biblical text.[150] A simple example of such typology might be: The Crossing of the Red Sea = deliverance from Egypt (literal) = rebirth in baptism (allegorical) = deliverance from sin (tropological/moral) = crossing the river of life and entering the heavenly Jerusalem (anagogical/eschatological). Or: Manna in the desert (literal) = Gift of the Eucharist (allegorical) = Wedding Feast of the Lamb (anagogical). Or: Ark of the Covenant (literal) = Mary, the Womb of God (allegorical) = New Jerusalem (anagogical). In each of these examples, we can see that the senses of Scripture presuppose and complement each others in differing ways. They comprise a network of reciprocally conditioning illuminations. The literal foreshadows and is fulfilled in the allegorical; the allegorical and tropological are mutually enhancing; the anagogical always "gathers up" and "brings to completion" the other typologies that have gone before. There is a mutual progression and fulfillment in all typology that enables the mystery of the Scripture to shine forth with its iridescent glory. The beauty of typology was summed up by St. Augustine when he said, "The New Testament is concealed in the Old, and the Old Testament is revealed in the New."[151]

*Anagogy* is the final and most powerful form of Scriptural typology. There is no better tool than "an anagogical sense of Scripture" to help us develop a comprehensive vision of the Christian faith. *Anagogy* is the perfection of typology because our union with Christ is ultimately realized beyond the Scripture itself. "We are not a people of the Book," the *Catechism of the Catholic Church* teaches.[152] The anagogical sense of Scriptural calls us to look to the heavenly Jerusalem as the fulfillment of the unfolding of God's Plan for salvation (Eph. 1:9). Cultivating an "anagogical imagination," we are led and "lifted up (*ana+agein*)" to

---

[150] Henri De Lubac, *Medieval Exegesis: The Four Senses of Scripture*, trans., Mark Sebanc (Grand Rapids, MI: William B. Eerdmans Publishing Company, 1998). For a less sophisticated, more popularized version, see Mark P. Shea, *Making Senses Out of the Scripture: Reading the Bible as the First Christians Did* (San Diego, CA: Basilica Press, 2004).

[151] St. Augustine, *Quaest. In Hept. 2,73: PL 34, 623*, cited in the *Catechism of the Catholic Church* #129

[152] *Catechism of the Catholic Church #108.*

contemplate, and participate in, the Wedding Feast of the Lamb. It is in the Wedding Feast of the Lamb that our Eucharistic ecclesial existence finds its ultimate end. We must cultivate a living anagogical sense if our lives are to "show forth" (proclaim), and strengthen, our participation in the Resurrection of Christ.

Because of the "wages of sin," it is difficult to express and maintain a vibrant anagogical vision in our faith and worship. Typology easily deteriorates into allegory. Here lurk the dangers of turning typology into prosaic system attempting to tame the mystery of Scripture. "Allegory," as one theologian has put it, "has historically been the death of mystagogy."[153] To live a fully Christian (anagogical) life, we must view typology, not as an interesting and traditional method for interpreting Scripture, but as a contemplative tool enabling us to enter more fully into the drama of our salvation. Scripture is trivialized when we become satisfied with interpretive clichés. Yes, "the Old Testament conceals the New," and the "New Testament reveals the Old." Yes, the events of the New Testament are "foreshadowed" in the Old, and the events of the Old Testament "find their realization" in the New. Yet, we are not "a people of the Book."[154] Scripture *as a whole* looks for an *extra-biblical* completion. Scripture is not self-contained, despite the many wonderful analogies and allegories that exist between the Old and New Testaments. Scripture culminates outside of itself in the Wedding Feast of the Lamb. It remains a dead letter if it is not constantly and effectively connected to the future reality of the heavenly Jerusalem.

The coinherence of the Old and New Testaments is, in its own way, a parallel mystery to the two natures in Christ, as well as to the mutual indwelling of the Persons of the Trinity. Typology reflects the hypostatic union of the two natures in Jesus and the *perichoresis* of the Trinity. It is meant to 'lift us up' into the Mystery of their respective reciprocities. Typology, therefore, must never be tamed by using it only as a technique. Typology culminates in *anagogy* (eschatology),

---

[153] Enrico Mazza, *Mystagogy* (New York, NY: Pueblo Publishing Company, Inc., 1989) 13.

[154] Catechism of the Catholic Church, #108.

otherwise its ultimate purpose is not achieved. Played as an exegetical game, typology prevents us from experiencing the perfection, both of Scripture and of liturgy in the Wedding Feast of the Lamb.

We must implore the Holy Spirit to engender and sustain in us a strong anagogical sense. He alone can rescue us from the entropy of a clichéd theological endeavor that thinks of Jesus' redemptive work of salvation (Paschal Mystery) as a bygone event, or pictures his 2nd Coming in Glory as a faraway future reality. Only the Holy Spirit can bring home to us the immediacy and multiform presence of Christ in His Church, as well as in the Heavenly Jerusalem.

The Holy Spirit recalls to us the three movements of Jesus Passage: (1) The Father sends His Son, (2) The Son assumes our flesh and our death, and (3) The Son brings us in Eucharistic communion back to the Father. He also reveals to us the three-fold deification we experience in the *Ecclesia*: (1) Prepared and converted by the Liturgy of the Word, (2) lifted up to the Father in Christ through the Eucharistic Anaphora, (3) becoming one flesh with the Savior in Holy Communion. Finally, He secures for us the three-fold moments of growth we experience as Christ's Mystical Body: (1) Birth and Initiation into Christ through Baptism, Confirmation, and Communion, (2) Victory over Sickness and Death in the Mysteries of Unction and Reconciliation, (3) Armed and equipped for Service in the Mysteries of Marriage and Holy Orders.[155] Each of these three-fold actions of Christ is envisioned in its unconfused unity through the illumination of the Holy Spirit. We look to the Holy Spirit to keep before us the centrality of the eschatological dimension of Jesus as Alpha and Omega.

It is the most delicate and important theological task to acquire a living sense of the anagogical end of Scripture and Liturgy. The final truth about Jesus is the truth of His *future* coming. Like the early Christians, we cry, "Maranatha!, Lord, Jesus, come in glory!" (Rev. 22:20). Jesus as Omega brings to completion the work of Jesus as Alpha. He does this in ways both continuous with, and incomparably

---

[155] This trinity of three-fold movements is described poetically by Corbon, *The Wellspring of Worship*, 99-111, 146-158.

greater than, the historical, Eucharistic, and ecclesial modes of His presence. Jesus is the Lord of Lords and the King of Kings. Only anagogically can we truly apprehend the mysteries of Scripture, Liturgy, and *Ecclesia* as resplendent with His Trinitarian glory. Only a sustained vision of the heavenly Jerusalem and the Wedding Feast of the Lamb enables us to perceive the eternal depths of the *Ecclesia de Eucharistia*.

Within this abiding eschatological perspective, the *Ecclesia* (Church) can now be experienced as the incarnation of the Wedding Feast of the Lamb in the midst of a history redeemed by Christ. The Eucharist can now be experienced as the Assembly of those participating in the eternal 8th Day of the New Jerusalem as it exists on earth prior to its final unveiling (apocalypse) when Jesus appears in glory. The sacramental economy and the economy of salvation receive their final perfection in the heavenly liturgy, the fullness of which is manifest today in the Divine Liturgy of the *Ecclesia de Eucharistia*.

The heavenly Jerusalem coming down to meet us in the Church is the eschatological fullness into which we are assimilated each time we celebrate the sacramental mysteries. We ask the Holy Spirit to develop within us a strong anagogical élan. We want to see the Lord of Glory as the *pleroma* (fullness) of the Crucified Christ. We await His *Parousia* as the fulfillment of His mission and Person. We worship Him as pre-existent *Logos,* as Jesus of Nazareth (history), as resurrected Lord, as ascended King, as Eucharistic Host, as Ecclesial *Corpus Mysticum,* and as He who "will come again in glory to judge the living and the dead." Ascending to the heavenly Jerusalem by way of anagogy, we commune with Him there mystically until He comes to gather us into His Kingdom "with power and might." When at last He appears in glory, he will find us ready and waiting for Him, having at every Eucharist remembered "the cross, the tomb, the resurrection on the third day, the ascension into heaven, the sitting at the right hand, *and the coming again in glory...*"[156] Always remembering the future, it is Jesus himself whom we recognize "in the breaking of the bread," (Lk. 24:35) as well as in our service of the "least of our brothers and sisters" (Mt. 25:40, 45).

---

[156] Eucharistic Prayer, Byzantine Rite.

# LEITOURGIA LIVED

*A*s "anointed ones" "in Christ" ("Christians") we are citizens of the heavenly Jerusalem and participants, even now, in the Wedding Feast of the Lamb. Through the priestly action of Jesus and the power of His Holy Spirit, we are, as St. Paul says, even now seated with Christ at the right hand of the Father in His glory (cf. Eph. 2:6). Our life "is hidden with Christ in God" (Col. 3:3).

Deification, as we have seen, is the perfection of being fully initiated and assimilated into Jesus. "That which is not assumed is not healed," the Fathers said. Enfolded into the Corporate Person of Christ through Word and Sacrament, we "become God" in Him. "The creature, having by deification become God, no longer displays any energy other than the divine...henceforth there is only God, because the whole of his being...enters into the being of his elect."[157] Already, here below, the human person "created anew in Christ," becomes one who is "risen again." Some of the Church Fathers spoke of a "little resurrection" manifest in every person incorporated into Christ. "The Word comes to dwell in the saints by imprinting on them in advance...the form of his future advent, as an icon."[158] In the miracle of divinization, the Holy Spirit transforms all that we are into Christ: body, soul, spirit, heart, flesh, as well as our relationships with others and with the world.

What does a deified life look like in practice? Divinization is not a miracle that works *ex opere operato*. It requires our full and free consent. No one enters the mystery of *theosis* without uttering, with the Blessed

---

[157] St. Maximus the Confessor, *Ambigua*, 7 (PG 91, 1076), cited in Clement, *The Roots of Christian Mysticism: Texts from the Patristic Era with Commentary*, 267.

[158] St. Maximus the Confessor, *Gnostic Centuries* II, 28 (PG 90, 1092), cited in Clement, ibid., 267.

Virgin Mary, a personal Fiat: "Let it be done to me according to Your Word" (Lk. 1:38). Our entire being is transfigured by the Holy Spirit through the *Corpus Mysticum* only if we consent to be flooded by the river of life (Rev. 22:1) flowing from beneath the Throne of the Lamb. By giving ourselves completely to participation in the divine *leitourgia*, we allow our identities be divinely transformed and our lives become "trees of life" capable of producing "fruits of the Spirit" in season and out (Rev. 22:2; 2 Tim. 4:2).

"Putting on Christ" (Rom. 13:14) is not a pious cliché meant as a metaphorical allusion. To "put on Christ" is to enter into the very Person of Jesus Christ. This does not mean thinking occasionally of the historical Jesus, paying lip service to the importance of keeping his commandments, or even "doing the best I can" to live up to his standards. Jesus is not primarily a teacher, and "putting on Christ" is never merely a matter of imitating his example. In our baptism we "put on Christ" that he might become the substance (form) of our life; that he might transform us into himself, without remainder, yet also without loss or confusion of our unique identities as persons. To "be," for a Christian, is to be "in Christ." No other kind of existence qualifies as "life." Assumed into Jesus, we become "partakers" of his divinity, and our human existence actualizes its created purpose. "Anyone who is in Christ," says St. Paul, "is a new creation; the old has passed away, behold, the new has come" (2 Cor. 5:17).

Christ also causes us to become "partakers" of his sinless humanity. To become deified is not only to "become God" in Christ; it is also to share increasingly in his humanity. Uniting us to his body in the *Ecclesia de Eucharistia*, the Son makes our humanity ever more like his own. Our life itself becomes a "eucharist" until His image in us is transformed into the likeness of Him who is the splendor of His Father. We are to have "the mind of Christ" (1 Cor. 2:16; cf. Rom. 12:2). Jesus is the only perfect human being. To be fully human, we must be one with Him in his humanity, especially in his *kenosis* (self-emptying) (Phil. 2:2-11) and His suffering (cf. Col. 1:24).

"In Christ" we live a *mystical realism*. If deification raises us to a level of "equality" with God, it does so for the purpose of loving Him as

He loves us, and of cooperating with Him in the salvation of others. Mission is always a defining by-product of divinization. "[M]an can and must find his identity in his mission. This mission is constitutive of the person within the mission of Christ."[159] The divine *leitourgia* draws us into itself "for the life of the world." We become co-redeemers with and in Christ.

It is not essential to understand exactly how our union with Jesus divinizes us. The important thing is to surrender ourselves completely to the mystery of deification and learn how to live as willing "partakers of the divine nature." In those deified in Christ, the Scripture and the liturgy become their life. The Garden is restored. Paradise is regained. The Eighth Day has dawned. The Heavenly Jerusalem has descended into our midst. The celebration of the Wedding Feast of the Lamb can already be heard. The Resurrection is manifest in the very bodies of those engrafted freely and fully into Christ. The action of God is inscribed in every facet of the person and their behavior. The faces of those given over to the miracle of *theosis* radiate the kenotic beauty of their crucified and risen Lord. The liturgy celebrated becomes the liturgy lived.

A *liturgy of the heart* is the end result of the *leitourgia* of the *Ecclesia*. The deification that Christ works within us transfigures and sets free every fiber of our being. The tiniest impulses of our nature seek fulfillment in the *communio* of the Blessed Trinity. Desire for anything is experienced as a desire for union with God. Suffering is experienced as an opportunity for anticipating our final sacrifice of surrender in gratitude to the One who made us in His own image and likeness.

At the same time, the process of *theosis* increases our kindness and self-possession. It returns us to ourselves, enabling us to view ourselves and others with the compassion of Christ. We look upon our own sins and those of others as the angels do: with relative indifference, save for the fact that, thanks to the grace of the divine Economia, the Lord

---

[159] Von Balthasar, *Theo-Drama: Theological Dramatic Theory IV: The Action*, trans., Graham Harrison (San Francisco: Ignatius Press, 1994) 62.

has used them to bind us more closely to Himself.[160] With St. Paul, we "rejoice in our weakness," for we recognize that "when we are weak, then we are strong" (2 Cor. 12:9-10) We know very clearly that "apart from Me, you can do nothing" (Jn. 15:4), but also that we "can do all things in Christ who strengthens" us (Phil 4:13).

Persons in *theosis* exercise a perpetual *epiclesis* [invocation of the Holy Spirit] on the altar of their hearts. It is as natural as breathing for them to call upon the Holy Spirit. They are acutely aware that "it is not I who lives, but Christ who lives in me" (Gal. 2:20). They also instinctively know that "the Spirit prays within them with sighs too deep for words" (Rom. 8:26). Their lives are a living liturgy. They live by and in the Holy Spirit. They live in oneness with Jesus, solely for the honor and glory of the Father. Theirs is a life of perpetual and joyful surrender. All traces of heteronomy are gone. They know in their very bones that in God's Will is their peace. Theirs is no longer a struggle to "do God's Will." They "thirst" to do God's Will. They have been given a share in the love that caused Jesus, swollen-tongued on the Cross, to utter the words, "I thirst" (Jn. 19:28). Pain (suffering) and joy are no longer mutually exclusive for them. They join the *Stabat Mater* (Mother of Sorrows) at the foot of the Cross. They assent freely, joyfully to the offering (sacrifice) of themselves with Jesus in His salvific act. Yet, they do not minimize the fact that it costs them "not less than everything." They have long ago stopped counting the cost of being surrendered to Jesus. They no longer kick against the goad (cf. Acts 26:14), as Paul did for so many years. They know Jesus' yoke is easy, his burden light (Mt. 11:30). They have learned through ascetic and contemplative experience that it is in his light that "they see light" (Ps. 36:9).

Persons who give themselves to the Trinity in this way "radiate a light that does not originate in them but shines from heaven through the word they have welcomed in faith."[161] They no longer have an external or extrinsic relationship with Jesus. They have "entered into him" so completely that, as St. John of the Cross says, they have moved

---

[160]  This is the view of St. John of the Cross. See his *Spiritual Canticle*, XX, 10.

[161]  Adrienne Von Speyr, *Man Before God*, (San Francisco: Ignatius Press, 2009) 36.

from "seeing God in others" to "seeing others in God."[162] The light of Christ illumines and warms everything they see and touch. It is as though such persons "unfold their branches, leaves, and flowers in the direction shown them by the light."[163] They are living embodiments of John's vision of the "trees of life, which bear twelve crops of fruit in one year, one in each month, and the leaves of which are the cure for the nations" (Rev. 22:2).

Being oriented this way by living in His Light is ultimate freedom. Persons divinized by the light of Christ are no longer afraid of making a mistake. They use no moral calculus to assess their relationship with God. They have learned through *ascesis* and contemplation that freedom means, as St. Bernard says, "being unable to will what is evil… and incapable of willing anything that is not desired by God."[164] They have abandoned the stoic theology that assumes that man's supreme perfection and happiness is something God wants to prevent him from attaining. All traces of heteronomy have disappeared. Conscience has replaced superego. They realize that everything is a gift of the Trinity for the fulfillment of the human person. They know God has created us to be happy, to share in His own *perichoresis*. They no longer feel the need to engage in theological litigation. They realize that everything is theirs precisely because everything is His (1 Cor. 3:23; cf. 2 Cor. 6:10). If it were not his, it could never be mine. If it could not be mine, He would not want it for Himself. Zero sum theology – and the convoluted, scrupulous psychology stemming from it – is rejected with finality. God is experienced as a God of abundance. The deified person knows that he or she is not trying to wrest from God something that the Trinity has not already been trying to return to humankind since the fall of Adam and Eve. They know from experience the truth of St. Irenaeus' words: "The glory of God is the human person fully alive."[165]

---

[162] St. John of the Cross, *Living Flame of Love*, IV, 5.

[163] Von Speyr, *Man Before God*, 36.

[164] St. Bernard, *Epist. Ad Fratres de Monte Dei*, II, n. 16, P.L. 184:349, quoted by Thomas Merton in *The Silent Life* (New York, NY: Dell Publishing Co., Ind., 1957), 35.

[165] St. Irenaeus, *Against Heresies*, IV,20,7 (SC 100 bis, p. 648), cited by Clement, *The Roots of Christian Mysticism: Texts from the Patristic Era with Commentary*, 265

Life in the Trinity is the purpose for which we were created. It is the motivation for the Incarnation and the miracle of Redemption. Entering the *Corpus Mysticum* of Jesus, we receive the *"theanthropic* life" of the Trinitarian *Communio Personarum*. No greater gift can be imagined than our deification in Christ. The Trinity is the Source, Goal, and Archetype of all human "being." "God himself is the life of those who participate in him."[166] No words can express the gratitude we owe Him for calling us out of darkness "into his marvelous light" (1 Pt. 2:9). No greater life can be conceived that the one we have been predestined to live from before the foundation of the world: life in the Trinity.

---

[166] St. Irenaeus, *Against Heresies*, V,7,1 (SC, p. 153,86-8), cited by Clement, ibid., 265.